VOYOVIC
BRIGITTE
and other stories

Modern stories of drug-taking, revolution,
migrant workers, prostitution, young men and women
— kindred spirits. An entertaining and disturbing
collection set among the subcultures of Europe.
A subtle interplay of personality, emotion,
place and idea. Unusual experiences,
acutely observed.

Niall Quinn received the 1983
Brendan Behan Memorial Fellowship award

VOYOVIC BRIGITTE
and other stories

Niall Quinn

WOLFHOUND PRESS

Published in paperback 1983
Wolfhound Press
68 Mountjoy Square
Dublin 1.

© 1980 Niall Quinn

All rights reserved. No part of this book may be reproduced or utilised in any form or by any means, electronic or mechanical, including photography, filming, recording or video recording, or by any information storage and retrieval system without prior permission in writing from the publisher.

British Library Cataloguing in Publication Data
    Quinn, Niall
    Voyovic & other stories
    I. Title
    823'.9' 1FS

ISBN 0-905473-61-2
ISBN 0-86327-016-6 Pbk

Typeset by Redsetter Ltd., Dublin.

This book is published with the financial assistance of The Arts Council / An Chomhairle Ealaíon, Ireland.

Contents

Voyovic	7
All to Nothing	24
Fixing	42
Fates	58
The Search	68
Marchpast	81
Brigitte	113

Voyovic

GASTARBEITER VOYOVIC IS DEAD. He died after leaving my room. I rolled the waxplugs in the sweat of my hands, plied them into my ears and in that artificial silence lay down to sleep.

The police knew; they shook my elbows, gestured and brought me naked down the corridors to the deathroom and its warm, dead body. Then a hot splurge of vomit rose and spewed out of my mouth. They pushed me to the shower-cubicle, took the hose from the peg and sprayed my face, forcing their fingers into the back of my mouth while the vomit poured out. When it was finished they asked 'Ja?'. I nodded and walked over to the body. The doctor shook three blue and yellow capsules into his hand, glanced at the police, then offered them to me. I bit them open in my mouth, already glazed and soulless, and slumped down to lie beside Voyovic's warm, dead body.

*

There is never silence in a Guestworkers' House. Doors are wrenched open, slammed shut; feet plod and tramp the stairs and corridors day and night; toilets flush endlessly, radios and televisions blare. And in their individual conclaves the voices of Europe's poor shout to the noise of bottles banging on tables, falling on floors. Or being hurled against the walls. Occasionally, or once a day, the shouts of a man in fear and disbelief as he tries to back out of a fight. Occasionally, or once a day, the high-pitched, confident voice of a whore as she mocks, cajoles and threatens for extra money. Or her terrified cries if she has misjudged; and the flat brutal sound of slapping hangs, then slaps again, against the noise of the house. Then the wait for that peculiar noise of police running up the stairs and through the corridors, and the bold, sure impersonal hustling of the protesting, struggling man out of the house. Then the finality of the housedoor slamming shut.

And still the noise continues, uninterrupted. Forever and ever that savage, wanton, joyless noise screams out from that doomed, homeless army of the European Guestworkers.

Voyovic ended his life in such a house. It was the slow, persistent creaking of the rope and the rhythmic sway of the body brushing with its death-silence against the partition wall that frightened a fellow Gastarbeiter in the next room. Each dreaded sway and groan penetrated deeper and deeper his Spanish indifference to noise. Then he panicked and ran from the room, out of the house, across the courtyard and out into the street to gesticulate frantically with trembling Spanish to a passing German. A group collected; someone understood. They took him to a *lokal*, fed him glasses of korn; another found the Housemaster, opened the door of Voyovic's room and found the body hanging from the ceiling.

Every army has its maimed and its wounded: every army honours its dead. Our army is no different. Our maimed are those who fell crippled from the scaffoldings, lost limbs and suffered their wounds in every industry of Europe in the blind, unconscious urge to be quicker and better than the native workers; the blind, unconscious urge to kill the aura of inferiority and begging vagrancy which is relentlessly shrouded upon us.

In our army, too, suicide is the final act of defiance, the last expression of contempt for surrender to an inferior, contemptible enemy. Voyovic died for a romantic notion.

*

I was sitting against a wall, smoking, at about 5 a.m. in the Rue Bourdan in Paris when Voyovic walked up and asked 'Workmobile?' I nodded. He sat and rolled a cigarette. We watched the empty, dark street; sensing the change of atmosphere. Finally he looked at me and said : 'Yugoslav.' We shook hands. 'Irish.' He smiled. Slowly, very slowly the morning began to show a glimmer of light and the workgroup collected in twos and threes patiently waiting for the company van to ferry us to factories and offices around Paris. When the van arrived and the worksheets handed out, Voyovic and I were paired and given a triangle of offices from Opera to Paix to the Rue Danielle. As always this meant drinking your own sweat in a frenzy of work before the office staffs started to arrive at 8 o'clock. Otherwise before you could get your hands on a machine its life history would be relentlessly repeated to you. And thus your chances of finishing the worksheet before noon and going onto bonus work were irreparably damaged.

Voyovic showed his experience immediately and six hours later we were almost finished. I was lying under a card punch machine, working and daydreaming, when the scent of danger came through as I heard Voyovic patiently explaining to a typist that one should not try to half-backspace on an electric in order to insert letters into mis-spelt words. He spoke slowly and clearly; and the typist kept repeating, in a slur of French, that she could not understand what he was saying. This reaction is not unusual in any country. It is endemic to the shoals of semi-literates from typists to barrowboys to the plainly chauvanistic. To all those of no notable intelligence when judged by their own crude manner of assessing people, not by the quality of their work, but by the social categories of their occupations. And of no notable brains when assessed by their devotion to this medieval criterion. The exceptions are rays of beauty, as was Monique, a student from Chartres who gave lessons in our Guestworker Hostel. With a radiance of mental health, her hands moving in a ballet of explanation, she effortlessly imparted the poise and poetry of her native language, and rallied our spirits to feel native, not step-children, to French. No taint of condescension, of intellectual slumming, ever marred her approach to us. Once, just once, the other side of her heart showed. She paused, looked around the bleakness of our messroom, looked at me, and asked: 'Is it really so lonely?' Her eyes held mine and her eyes held not compassion, but rage, clear translucent rage: don't accept it, don't let it cripple your dignity, fight back. Fight! I tried to look away but her eyes held. I looked down at my twisting hands, desperately searching for a way of answering truthfully without admitting that it dumbed me with pain. 'But Miss,' I answered 'It is always difficult for a grown man to say yes to a young girl.' She paused, then understood, and her Gallic humour soared into laughter.

I remembered, and smiled as I slid from under the machine to watch Voyovic. I only knew his name, and now wanted to see if he would accept the Guestworker's role of submission that the clerk was demanding of him.

Voyovic shrugged, went behind the typist's chair, and put his hands over her shoulders onto the machine to demonstrate. This is the best compromise we can offer, to introduce the comedy of Sesame Street into the situation and de-fuse it. I started to laugh, to help the situation, when the woman arose in a rigidity of outraged abruptness. Voyovic, startled, stepped back from her wrath. 'You mustn't dare touch me!' was exactly what she said. Then she added the precise word: 'Scum.'

Voyovic's skin tightened, and the beauty of a noble statue appeared on his face, held immobile by shock and pain. I walked over, afraid to touch him, knowing I would have to protect the clerk and thereby Voyovic. Thereby myself, for I know the greatest fear of our army, the fear we whisper to the new recruits: say goodbye when the police take you out of a confrontation with the natives. A gesture of explanation, the swing of a baton. A broken arm. And a man who must alone care for himself night and day is a cripple. No longer a worker and immediately you are nothing. Work registration cards – not work permit cards – withdrawn. And to cover the swing of the baton the police must charge you. And the crippled, unworkable guest is deported back to his nominal country where he is now no longer unstrange, no longer native, to that country which was first to ignore his quest for a better life and left him to fare as best he might in any foreign country that might have him.

The clerk sat primly, righteously self-vindicated in the Loudunite world of her own fantasy.

Voyovic's eyes flicked once over mine. He knew. I squeezed his shoulder, still rigid as steel. 'Christ,' I said 'They'd have cheered and lined the streets, again, Aryan, if you had occupied that colossal virginity, again.' Voyovic looked at me without smiling, and slowly nodded his head. Then the woman was primly walking, then running, towards a glassed-off manager's annex at the far end of the office. We started to collect our equipment. The manager arrived. Our company had been informed; we were to leave the premises 'instantly'. He tried to continue speaking, gave up, gestured his arms in the air like an ape, and while his simian play of flesh to flesh struggled to humiliate us the colours of the office staff began to emerge. Some winked, from behind his back, others stared out of the windows or straight at the ceiling. The rest tensed, ravenously, to enjoy the sacrifice for its blood taste, or for their primitive class honour and a strictly administered reminder to obey the rules of the status quo. First he told Voyovic not to lounge against the equipment. Voyovic ignored him. Then I was to sit while he ranted off the consequences of our behaviour. I ignored him and continued packing. A situation others would have dismissed with a wave of the hand towards the door and a compensatory shrug of the shoulders became, for him, a challenge to his integrity. Not to lounge: and you are reduced to an errant schoolboy. Sit: and you are reduced to childhood. Once his ridiculous, pre-emptory orders are disobeyed, everything else becomes a taunt to his manhood. His voice became shrill. He shouted that we were ungrateful to the 'Mother of our prosperity'. Voyovic laughed, then turned, quickly unzipped his fly, pulled his trousers and undershorts down to his ankles, bent over and said through his legs: 'To you and your connection with the mother of my prosperity'.

A few obedient clerks remained sombre-faced. But giggles and guffaws callously broke out from the rest. The man was now speechless. I finished packing: Voyovic pulled his trousers up and we started for the door. I held the door open for Voyovic to exit first. He paused and turned to stare at the manager, the well of hatred and contempt between them palpable in the air, each straining to strike, each holding the other's eyes in a bond of challenge to strike first. In the silence it produced, Voyovic's whisper fell; at once a gauntlet and a coup de grace. 'Remember! Debray was also a Jew, you Nazi sow.'

The man froze, stunned: a look of pained anguish sweeping across his face as if he now, and suddenly, understood the reptilian greed and obscenity, the reptilian nature, of his play for dominance over us. He was old enough to remember the existence of the French run camp at Le Vernet, and remember, too, the words used by the French to justify its existence and describe its Jewish and non-Jewish occupants: The Scum of the Earth. The scum of the earth sucking the lifeblood of France. And now he plainly knew he too belonged to those who, with deathcamps and nothing less, would boast, years later, that the trains ran on time.

Moments later we were down the stairs and bustling along the street to the first cafe. I looked at Voyovic. He was as tall as I, but blond and blue-eyed. He drew his finger across his throat and shrugged, mournfully. I tried to push away the listlessness of being jobless by ordering a beer; and ended up draining glass after glass of foamy, pale, weak lager while Voyovic, pushing away his own ghost, pounded the pinball flippers continuously and swore at the machine.

I was tasting the listlessness, the inadequateness, the homelessness as I had tasted it so often before. In cities and towns in Ireland, Israel, Norway and France I had supped from this cup. And finally, now, the sense of bereavement at losing yet another country, losing another attempt to establish my life. I knew, very clearly, that only in a slump of defeat and resignation could I continue to live in France. France had not changed; but it had changed me. I was tired of its streets and tired of its customs, as I had tired of all the streets and customs in all the countries I had known.

Customs turn sour, rot, turn to worms, and paralyse. They eat their way through the society until the signs of decay are visible on every street, their decadence of spirit as visible as sores in its culture and politics.

Voyovic crossed to refill his glass. 'Tomorrow,' he said, 'Tomorrow.' And I knew immediately the sad imminence of events: street, house, suitcase, railway station, another city, street, house, re-opening suitcase, repeating again and again in all the years ahead. Strike camp, break camp. And I wearied, suddenly, of all the battles I had lost.

*

At the time I was born there was one Jewish street in Dublin: Bloomfield Avenue. I was born at the top of it, and one day in my formative years I stood sheltered under the mothering arms of Mrs. Woolfson as the silent, electric van of the Swastika Laundry crept, stealthily, and obscenely as the swollen head of a bodyless snake, past the concrete air raid shelters in the middle of the road. No one, anywhere, threw a stone at the massive swastikas emblazoned on the sides and roof. Now I finally understood why, as I knew I was tired of Voyovic, for starting yet again the endless procession of disruption and enforced wandering.

It is a long time since I packed or unpacked a suitcase. I merely open it, live out of it, then close it a minute before the time comes for the next journey. Too optimistic, always, to believe I would live long in the bedsitters, the kibbutzim, the studios; or any of the human pens where the poor live. Then, overnight, too pessimistic to believe I would ever escape from them or could ever live, as a human being, in them. To live, meaning not to exist, but to be. Now the rally that Monique had stirred in me had been doused by Voyovic's casual acceptance of the realities, and his mournful awareness of the consequences of ignoring them.

Our credentials were well established as clients of the bar and so we were permitted to use the telephone. The Manager was 'occupied' but his secretary told us: 'Dismissal. Pay and papers ready for collection. Return test equipment and tools.' Another Voyovic shrug. He looked down at his glass. 'We have each other.' he said.

We paid and left, took a bus to the Workmobile office in Clichy, then went together to collect our belongings from our different hostels. Together, we each forfeited, as we had each forfeited before in other cities, our deposits of one month's rent — in lieu of quitting notice. While Paris, and the other cities, teemed with those just one kick short of the gutter obliged and ready to tramp the streets in search of just such cubicles of miserable living-space.

We bought two bottles of whisky at the Gard du Nord, found a bar at the end of one of the streets opposite where we could sip beer and lace it, secretly and liberally, with splashes of whisky. I had a little over twenty thousand francs; Voyovic a few thousand more. We both knew it was useless, footloose money. In our nominal countries, before we became strange and no longer at home there, such wealth could have been the beginning, the foundation, of prosperity. Even the poorest and dimmest at home had, over the years, accumulated the artefacts of a stable existence in which they could mature and grow, had spread the roots of years throughout their communities, were held and supported by that, given then that chance to branch out and flourish. But we had grown oddly, from force of circumstance, and would never take root in any society except our own, individual, solitary existence. We were footloose forever. A future of arrivals in grey, heart-stripped railway stations awaited us; and the cold, dark mornings in strange cities as we searched the streets of tenement buildings for lodgings; and seeing, against the dawn, that city's decay, visible on every other street. Yet if we returned to our nominal societies, our foreign touches, our no longer native ways, shook a nervous tremble from the web of relationships our erstwhile playmates of childhood had built for themselves in ways which were foreign, strange, and nerve-touching to our understanding.

We drank and talked. Voyovic had worked at home in Yugoslavia, then Italy, Austria, Switzerland, Holland and France. Between us we were just about out of countries. We laughed, banged our glasses on the table, called for more, sang the praises of La France, my heart, oh, my heart, to the cautious, wary barmaid. Oh, La France, our unwed mother; and the beauty of Paris and its chic, bedsitter pens, its perfumed exhaust fumes, its pleasant gendarmes armed with rifles and cruising the streets in wire-protected military tenders. Oh, La France, and its great literature of butterflies and dilettantes rivalling its cuisine and drenched in the same sauce, to protect the innocent. And the magnificent seal of French civilisation: the crossed blades of the guillotine. The barmaid smiled. 'You know France well.' 'Oh yes, very well,' we answered. She smiled again. 'And when are you going back to your own beautiful country?' She asked. 'When my heart' answered Voyovic 'loses its pity for the stupid.'

It was enough. Our anger passed, and we settled down to getting drunk in a melancholy and steadfast manner; and slowly, very slowly, with the aid of the barmaid, the memory of Monique and many friends, we made our peace with France, before we left.

At Dover the next morning the immigration officers took us aside and quizzed us about pay and conditions 'over there'. I thought they wanted to emigrate. Only Voyovic, burdened in Western Europe by the Hammer and Sickle on his passport, realized they were expertly checking our bona fides. Then the desolation of Victoria Station. Our fellow passengers decamped from the boat-train into the empty station; then, in minutes, the crowd thinned and disappeared. To where I have no idea. Everything was closed, even the subway, and a small group of desolate travellers, overburdened with suitcases, waited silently in a line at the kerb of the empty, deserted street. Voyovic looked uneasy and nervous. It was ominous. We crossed the forecourt to the arc-shaped street opposite. Still no sign of life. We crossed onto a main road and walked to the first corner, then turned to start tracking a route back to the station. Eventually, in a decaying side street, we found a cafe open. It was owned and staffed by Italian immigrants. After a ritual of recognition and introduction, Voyovic and they began an exchange of information. The lie of the terrain was explained and then, as blood knows blood, we were invited to sit in the warmth at the back. We learnt the range of payrates, accommodation-rates, the routes to follow through the bureaucratic maze of registering for work, the names of the industrial areas, and the oddities and tricks of accommodation agencies.

We stayed and ate, and waited for the evening papers which were due at 10 a.m. We sat. Time passed. Even Voyovic and the Italians ran out of conversation. Then we paid, tipped, and made our way back to the station.

The forecourt was thronged with immense, interchanging shoals of anonymous people, an overpowering amount of people parted only by the high, intruding buses. We waited by the newspaper stand and excused our presence by buying yesterday's Irish and Yugoslavian newspapers. It was odd, eerie, reading, like reading a letter addressed to someone else, someone who was loved by the writer. And we were prying, out of a childish loneliness on the daily intimacies, pleasant and unpleasant, of a cohesive family. But the cause of their love and the source of their strength for and with each other remained a half-remembered mystery. We put them down together and waited quietly.

The newspaper advertisements directed us only to agencies. We selected the only one that had included its address, and Star Flats were located in Kensington High Street. Everyone we asked told us to take the 'tube'. But among the sacred superstitions and other irrationalities developed by wandering both Voyovic and I dreaded travelling on underground systems. Everyone knew that a bus went from Victoria to there: but no one knew which one. After an hour and three buses later we arrived at Star Flats. A placard outside read: Short, long lets. Foreign and overseas visitors welcome.

Inside we found two tawdry, white-washed rooms; and two girls seated behind desks in each. Each looked pleasant, calm and cosmopolitan. I selected one, by instinct, and approached. 'Good morning.' I was right. When she replied the soft, Irish accent was unmistakable. Then I explained what we wanted; and she, with a graceful, casual elegance, nimbly flicked a form from a stack on her desk, placed it in front of me, and began to speak in a slow, didactic manner. 'Here. Your names. Write your names here. In big letters. Capital letters. Not small. Big.' I glanced at Voyovic seated beside me. He couldn't understand a word, but he shrugged and smiled. I looked at the girl. 'Your names. Your last names,' she continued. I misunderstood. 'She thinks we're using aliases,' I said to Voyovic. He blinked; and immediately his unique combination of opportunism and insight caught a solution. 'We'll use the same family name,' he said; 'She's British, remember. Tell her we're brothers.' 'She's Irish.' I explained. He shrugged: 'It's too simple.' Then he leaned back in his chair and lost all interest in the proceedings. The girl was using the top of her pen to indicate where I should write. 'Now Hotel. Where you live. Hotel. Name. Understand? Where you live.' I glanced up, puzzled, and caught her eye. She instantly smiled: soft, gentle, alluring. I smiled back. 'I'm Irish, too.' Her pose across the desk went rigid. 'But this agency is only for foreign, overseas visitors.' Her voice shrilled. I felt Voyovic beside me tense. 'We are foreign, from overseas, and visitors.' I was angered, slightly angered, but I knew it showed on my face. I felt I was being humiliated by a worthless enemy. Her voice rose higher: 'You are not a foreigner and you're . . . you're . . . you are *not* a visitor. AND,' she pre-emptorily concluded: 'WE CAN'T HELP YOU.'

I tried to protest, feeling the situation had been unjustly reversed, that I was the one seeking a fee in this miserable charade of business, supplicating that it should continue — 'But, Madam, you misunderstand, that is not true.'

She snatched and crumpled the application form: 'Look, Paddy, if you don't understand I haven't the time to explain.' She tossed the crumpled form under the desk. Her manner dismissed me and any appeal I might make. Nothing moved; no one spoke. I felt my body heave for breath and the sound of the biro breaking in my hand. Then Voyovic's fingers grasped my shoulder. I turned, as stunned as a baited bull. 'It's why the British win their wars,' he said, 'They make their cannon fodder thick.'

He had almost hit the mark; almost diverted, enfranchised, my anger into laughter. I heard a telephone being raised and, twice, the swish of the dial revolving. But it would only take a minute to kill this bitch, and more than a minute before police arrived; less than a minute to expunge her degrading, inhuman existence from my consciousness. Then Voyovic spat into the coleen's face; and the edge of madness left my mind. We walked peacefully from the office. At peace forever with each other. All debt between us, even that to be contracted in the future, had been acknowledged, and repaid. It was resurrection and life.

*

A taxi driver took us to a central area of shabby, disused, derelict streets and a bar, like the streets, where the dirt and scavengering cheapness were rendered more obscene by the artificial light of glittering neon blinking into the morning. We paid to enter the bar. It was, our driver-friend told us, one of the few places in London where we could get a drink at that time. On a stage at the back of the bar a plain, flabby, graceless girl danced a striptease with all the sensibility of a monkey admiring itself. We ignored the circus and drank until the regular bars finally opened. Then we had to buy some bottles when we learned they were going to close again in the afternoon.

That evening we took the train to Harwich and the ferry back to the mainland. The immigration officers at the Hook of Holland asked us where we were going and waved us through when we said Hamburg. At the German border they checked passports, asked no questions, and we arrived in Hamburg at 3 p.m.

Within the hour we had met Anja. Dark-haired, alluring, pale beautiful Anja with the albumen-white eyes. We had wandered out from the station and stopped at an Imbiss for coffee. She served us, smiled at Voyovic from under long, blinking, melancholy eyelashes, and refused the tip. Moments later a green and white police car stopped outside, and one of the officers came in. He had a green jacket and fawn trousers and I had to look twice to recognise it for a uniform. He smiled and said goodday to us, then turned and ordered two take-out snacks. He was about my age and I wondered, as I looked at his back, if he too had a memory littered with sharp, glass fragments of childhood. Anja fumbled as she pressed the take-out box into shape. She looked up at me, discarded the box for another, quickly pressed it out, filled it and handed it to the officer. There had been fear in her eyes. I exchanged glances with Voyovic. He had noticed it too. The officer left and Anja stood, her mouth slightly open, one small fist nestled at the side of her mouth and her eyes, unblinking, staring at the police in the car outside. Then she looked to me and said, very quietly, venomously: 'I HATE THEM.' The police were eating and licking their fingers, a la television. I nodded.

Voyovic hunched over the counter and began to explain our need for information. Anja 'phoned a guesthouse in Osterstrausse, confirmed they had vacant rooms, then explained to us how to get there and book-in. Next morning we had registered our address, received two months' permits from the Immigration Office, taken our medicals, gone through the labyrinth of the Labour Office, found jobs and opened yet again our suitcases. And all this with the sisterly care of Anja.

I had been desperate to re-settle, and the first evening home from work, knowing I could handle the job comfortably, knowing I had, in the last country I had thought imaginable, taken root, I went to the Reeperbahn alone and got so totally drunk that I slept in the bar and had to return to work the next morning unshaven and unwashed. No one minded. An invisible weight lifted from my shoulders. For the first time in my life I was breathing the air of freedom. That evening Voyovic came to my room. His eyes were quick, alert, sensible. Too much so. He looked drawn and tired and stumbled a little, but the outward appearance of drunkenness was held in check with a visible and brutal determination. We sat at the window overlooking the courtyard, with two squat, fat bottles of Italian red wine at our feet. I tried, half-heartedly, some conversation, but Voyovic would only nod or shrug in reply. The drink, and the amount we had been drinking, frightened me. It would be too easy to forget perpetually the realities, and the opportunities, in this endless dullness of alcohol.

We sat and listened to the noise of the house. I wouldn't be here long. I could sense an avenue of escape opening for me. The evening passed and Voyovic, now too drunk to walk, mutely, mournfully, lay down on the bed and slept. I stayed awake an hour longer, gazing into the wine in my glass, sipping it, trying to recognise, to plan, the outlines of the future. I would find an apartment in Altona, the old part of Hamburg, where the ancient streets were woven in a lace of sculpture and art; and in the alcoves above each doorway the canephores, missing wings, or arms, or heads, were abstracts of a nameless urge in me. They touched, awakened, a long, long-lost part of me; and I had only to stroll in those streets to feel a hidden past in me come alive. Two minutes away, in the reconstructed Altona, in the bright arcades of shops and restaurants and new houses, the variety of nationalities and languages, the mosaic culture, was a bazaar of palpable happiness to me. Anja lived in old Altona, near the park and the grim, huge, impregnable, concrete bombshelter. A landmark for memories, and a dreadful warning; and memories and warnings too in the bomb-ripped streets, now conspicuously patched with rebuilt houses, built between their spared neighbours, their modern fronts flushed into the old facades: the death-dance scars of the bomb-run lines brutally stamped through the area, to converge on the harbour two miles away.

Coming home the next afternoon I stopped at the Imbiss. Anja was bright, vivacious and brimming with radiance. I wanted to enrol at the People's Institute for language and history lessons. Anja 'phoned for me and arranged the appointment. Casually, she asked after Voyovic. First his health, then immediately changed to ask about life in the hostel; then mentioned Voyovic's appetite and left a question-mark hanging in her tone — then switched again to schools and learning. 'No one can take away what you have in your head.' She repeated it. Her family were Altoners as far back as anyone knew. She knew, in her blood, that fate could frown and all would be lost 'except what you have in your head'. Anja spoke German, French and English fluently, had a diploma in shorthand-typing, a certificate in nursing, and was now serving time in the Imbiss towards a chef's diploma. After that she wanted to find something else, perhaps flying, but it was expensive and of no great utility. Perhaps mechanics. That was useful. Anja was twenty-two years old. She wanted, with a gentle, fierce longing, a security not based on money or political creeds, but on her proven ability and confidence in herself. Then she asked, as her mouth hung slightly open, girlishly, if Voyovic went with many girls. I shook my head. 'I don't understand.' She said, in sadness and bewilderment, then paused: 'I wish my father were still alive.'

I began the prelude to leaving. Gently, as if speaking of holy things, ignoring my preparations, she told me she went to Catholic church each Sunday, then walked to the cemetery and spent an hour, sitting on a bench near her father's grave. Her eyes opened to me: 'Would you like to come with me, please?' she asked.

We waited for her outside the church. She came out, buttoning her speckled-grey overcoat, hiding bashfully under its broad, raised collar, a little girl seeming strange and flattered at being so grown-up. We walked to her home. Occasionally she laughed, nervously and tense. Impetuously, as we entered the hall, she put her arms around Voyovic and kissed him. He was rigid, ungainly, and out of place. He seemed more humbled than encouraged. Anja had a large picnic hamper prepared and now carried it under her arm so naturally, so at ease with it, that I could feel the gladness of her heart. We walked on, past a huge old building that was once a Gestapo headquarters and now, ironically, a registry office; past the brewery, across Stressemannstrasse and then down the almost country roads to the cemetery. We bought flowers at the gate and entered. Anja passed the basket to me and we followed her. At each Jewish grave on the route to her father's she stooped, knelt, laid the open palm of her hand face downwards on the earth, then rose and walked on. She prayed at her father's grave while we stood behind. She cleaned a small plaque lying beside the headstone with her hands and beckoned us forward. A memorial stone, identical to thousands of others in the graveyard, to commemorate a soldier's unrecovered body.

A little further on we found the bench and settled around it. To sit upon it seemed unnatural. Anja unwrapped the sandwiches and poured tea, happily preoccupied. We ate and talked, of the sadness of being human and the savageness of humanity. I rested my head against the bench. The dead have always, from somewhere in the universe, haunted me; and death, not for its extinction, but its indifference to our understanding, troubled me. It can only be as dreamless, perpetual sleep. Only now are we, oddly, more than the sum of our parts; in death merely equal, yet still intrinsic to the universe. I slept. I awoke to Anja's delighted laughter as the lithe, lean Voyovic chased her around headstones. I closed my eyes. I had seen Voyovic's hesitancy. And also his willing eagerness. But not the ghost which lay between. We stayed a few hours more and then it was time to go. And time for me to leave them alone. I returned to the hostel and tried to occupy my mind with a grammar, encouraging myself by occasionally glimpsing at my dreams. Then I gave in. I went to the nearest Imbiss and bought a bottle of whisky. I wanted Voyovic and Anja to marry, to settle, to have children. Then I could be a friend. The agony was the meantime when I would be in a limbo, neither friend nor stranger nor lover to either while we were together; and, unwillingly, strangely devisive when with either one alone. It was time to leave them both. I sipped the whisky and watched the courtyard, heard the noise of the house. Life was being, despite this gentle sorrow, kind to me. I sipped and dreamed away my future to the day they would carry me, dead, to that cemetery. And the use I would put myself to meantime. Work provided money and that, almost automatically, all my needs. I had no great ambitions, no belief in any cause. I lived on time's wings and believed they would bring me to a purpose or not. I had no need to ask an excuse for my existence or call it by another name.

Voyovic, stooped and bent over like an old man, walked across the courtyard, a parcel under his arm. I waited. And waited. He entered the room, wordlessly placed the packet on the window sill and sat down to mutely stare at the evening sky. 'I'm sick,' he said, 'She knew the first time. I'm sick.' He reached, took a bottle from the parcel and filled a glass of whisky. I waited, waiting as long as I could before I spoke: 'You're a liar, Voyovic.' I pushed his shoulder. He laughed and drained the glass. 'You know too.' 'Marry her, Voyovic.' He refilled his glass and drank. 'I have shamed myself' he said and drained the whole glass, painfully, with effort. 'You couldn't. She loves you.' He stopped, his hand halfway to the bottle. 'That's it.' He said: 'She tried. I couldn't. You know why?' Again he refilled his glass. I was relieved. I wanted him to drink himself to sleep in the chair. I knew the answer: knew the cause and the cure. Years of wandering in countries that were, to us, virtual labour-camps; the bitter, barren months of longing, the despairing nights of drunkenness, the surrender to the parodies offered by prostitutes, the loveless, animal jerkings mocking and crippling us to escape back to work, and work, and work, without hope of ever, in the stream of the native society, finding acceptance with the plague-bell of the transient worker ringing in our every word and gesture; too foreign to the women of our own class, and too far, far, below the aspirations of the rest. The noise of the house hushed outside the shell of our intimacy. I held his hand. In some long forgotten, ancient way, we communicated. And the sounds of the Turks, the Yugoslavs, the

Spaniards, the Gabonese, the North Africans, even, somewhere in the house, the high-pitched, tense accents of East German refugees, fell muted, denied their force, against the shell we had formed against the world.

'I love her,' he said. I nodded. 'And you?' he asked: 'You love her too?' A heartbeat passed. 'Yes. I love her too.' He seemed relieved. 'Then it is good.' He clinked his glass with mine and smiled. 'Lostrovia!' The whisky disappeared, rapidly, from the first bottle. Voyovic staggered over to the shower cubicle and threw-up. He came back, shouted 'LOSTROVIA!' and gave me a Russian bear-hug. Then he searched in the parcel, found a bar of chocolate, divided its cubes into the two glasses and refilled them with whisky. It was hard, a punishment, to drink more. I forced the whisky past my lips. Voyovic watched me. 'You want to sleep?' 'No, no.' 'LOSTROVIA!' He shouted again the Russian toast, drank. His eyes looked up to mine: 'It is good that we met,' he said. 'We cannot lose each other again.'

I tried to find words, to reason, to prise open the shell of understanding so that we could each, finally, know the other. It seemed possible, in that dull, bright haze of whisky, seemed obvious. But vanished everytime I reached to touch, and seemed, then, unimportant, leaving me drunkenly staggering between question and answer, blearily, wondering which was which, then angrily dismissing it all, then straightening, looking around, wondering what I had been searching for. Voyovic was watching me. He laughed. I laughed. We drained and refilled our glasses, fished out cubes of chocolate and fed them to each other, laughing and punching. For a moment I knew. I grew serious. My head fell to nodding profoundly with wisdom; Voyovic's nodded too. We looked at each other's nodding with all the serious sensibility of monkeys, then exploded into shrieks of laughter. We grew quiet. It was important to hold onto this night, these moments of understanding and the solitude of ourselves. My eyes closed. Voyovic shook me awake. We shook hands. Raised our glasses in toast. Then he left, suddenly, quickly, wordlessly, and the peace and solitude immediately shattered into unbearable, ragged, cutting noise. I drank, swallowed and swallowed again, and the noise in this loneliness ripped open my mind in shreds of trembling, quivering shivers of tears. In soulless desperation I warmed the wax of the earplugs in the sweat of my palms; and plied it into my ears.

*

Voyovic left no relatives, except me. An official asked me some questions, then asked me to leave the room. Their deliberations took almost all day, then a police officer came out, apologised, and explained the verdict of suicide and its implications. Involuntarily I winced each time he said the word. I signed some papers. They gave me a chit to collect his belongings from the police station. There they gave me his suitcase and an envelope of money, plus a list of expenses they had been obliged to deduct from his savings. An officer in civilian clothes took me aside and explained that there would be difficulties in renewing my work-registration. He apologised, shook my hand, wished me good luck. I took the suitcase and walked on. I came to St. Pauli, the area of prostitutes and pimps, of perversion and despair, and the eternal Salvation Army group on the corner calling for God's mercy. I explained, as best I could, to one of its girls, that my friend was dead. His belongings were in the suitcase. I had no use for it. She took the suitcase and moved into the centre of the group. She came back and took my hand. 'We are going to pray for your friend' she said. And there, on the corner of the Reeperbahn and the Davidstrasse, they sang a hymn for Voyovic. I gave her his money and left.

There was no ceremony at the Crematorium. They explained that no coffin would be used. I again identified the body, a last chance to kiss the hand clenched over the left forearm. Fifteen minutes later they gave me the remains in a small, silverpapered box. A tag clipped to the corner read: 'Voyovic, Mladin. 1953-1978'. I offered it Anja. She lowered her head and walked away. I walked to the harbour. At Landungsbruecken I found some steps leading down to the water. I squatted and put my hand in. It was cold, very cold. I looked up. Across the harbour tugboats and barges churned by. Beyond them grim, dull warehouses with washed-blue, almost green, slate roofs. I walked back up the steps and walked on, holding the silver box in my hands. Derelict men squatted in doorways around the area. I crossed the road and walked into a bar. It had an Imbiss at the front and, behind that, a scattering of wooden benches and tables. More derelicts lay around, men and women, some sleeping, some drunk, all covered in stale, derelict grime. I asked for a coffee and a whisky, took them over to a bench and sat. Then I opened the silverpapered box, cupped it to my mouth, and ate the remains.

*

At Dublin Airport the room-finding service booked me into a hotel. The streets looked unfamiliar, strange and foreign. It had been many years. I drank a little in the hotel bar. The barman tried to make conversation, then gave up. I went to my room and slept. When I awoke it had grown dark. I went to the window to look across Drumcondra Road and the lights of Dublin. Diagonally across from the window I saw a small neon sign. It read: 'SWASTIKA'. And underneath, the words 'Dry Cleaning'.
    beat.

All to Nothing

IT SEEMED REASONABLE. They made everything seem reasonable. They could have you flogged and make it seem reasonable. In fact they often did. It was their nature.

Kempler walked down the road, the sounds in his mind lisplessly cursing them in strings of strange, oathless words. He started to climb a tree on the river bank, shimmying-up it, his legs wrapped tightly around the trunk. He felt the sensation, felt and wondered a moment, then slid down to the ground, guiltily.

There wasn't much to do between now and nine o'clock. He didn't have a watch but it'd been ten to five when she squeezed, in her boundless generosity, the five tenpenny pieces into his hand. She had rubbed the back of his head and smiled down to his level: there's a good boy.

Kempler re-crossed the road. Even when they smiled you still knew you were being flogged, but gently. Dissension would bring a flat open hand to punish ingratitude in the presence of the first arriving office colleagues, their ohs and hand-to-mouth intercessions adding an extra smack to the humiliation of pain.

He knocked at the door. Hypocrites. They did the same. They tingled with delight in their intercessions. It was their bloody nature.

He lounged at the gate. Mrs. Roche opened the door. Michael was having his tea and his father wouldn't let him out afterwards.

But it was a pain anyway to be in their presence. Their bulbous bodies, their embrocative, sickly-sweet smell. And there was going to be something like twenty of them that night in the house. Wandering the streets was better.

Go down to the church and say a Rosary, they said, then go to the pictures. He said the Rosary and put the beads back in his pocket. There were only two women in the church and they were up front near the altar rails. If only they'd leave. He promised God he'd say another Rosary if they left. They stayed. Then he made an offer God couldn't refuse: he'd put the fifty pence in the poorbox if they left. But then flocks of them would be back for Benediction at eight o'clock and he'd have to walk the streets penniless until the house was clear. It was too late. Nothing to do but hold your promise and offer up the added inconvenience as well.

It wasn't accepted. He stayed in the peace of the church and rubbed the timber of the prayer-rail with his hand. Then he suddenly bored of it all and left.

Outside the Spring air was soft and mild. The scones at tea had been nice. They'd even let him eat with his usual gusto without their usual upbraidings. He should have put some in his pocket. They'd have let him away with it, tonight. They were being reasonable. Maybe that was what the Doctor had meant. It was give and take. All perfectly natural. And in a few weeks after this evening's party his sister would be married and there'd be one less of them.

Two women stood at the corner. In Dublin's sprachgefuehl slang, with its relish of marrying the word to the object, they were *auldwans*. One was shabbily huge with wads of fat and the other, yet with massive, broad hips, was shabbily thin, like a well-used cane, in comparison. Two *youngwans* scampered around them. They couldn't run properly, but jerked and showed their hairless, pimply legs confidently. Maybe the doctor would understand that. That would revolt anyone. But you couldn't tell everything to the doctor. He was married to one of them. But it was still strange that he understood so much even before you said it. He even knew that Kempler wouldn't have been let near him if it hadn't been for that 'wan' who was a nurse and never even asked him before she started to unbutton his shirt.

But that was their nature with little boys. They find it hard to take their hands off you. They're just being affectionate, the doctor said. And Kempler didn't tell him that he didn't like to be pawed. And he didn't like being sent to a doctor 'cos there was nothing wrong with *him*. The doctor became grave, even stern, and pointed at him with his pencil. 'I can't help you if you lie to me. Now you *did* strike that nurse, didn't you?'

That was the problem. To them. That was the only problem to them. Take off your shoes and stockings. Walk across the room. Come back. Walk across the room again and keep your arms outstretched. now turn. Close your eyes and walk over here. KEEP YOUR ARMS

OUTSTRETCHED!'

Very good.

Then her fingers, working with the nimble, disquieting touch of centipedes, started to unbutton his shirt. He pushed her away and stepped back. She grabbed his hand, pulled him close, and slapped his arm. The cheek of you. His fist swung and punched her in the face. That was the problem. That's not give and take. No, said the doctor, not even if you include the flogging that came later. And that wasn't the right word. A caning is different.

But you can't cane with a flog, said Kempler. That isn't the problem, said the doctor. You have a grudge against people, especially women. That's the problem.

Kempler looked past him at the wall. They're too clever. Better say nothing. Then the doctor told him he mustn't sulk. Everyone lies to themselves. Few are lucky to have a doctor to stop them growing up because of that in a snarled, twisted, perhaps crippled, manner. They just lead their lives as grown-up children, trapped and still believing their own lies.

Most of them? asked Kempler. Yes, most of them I'd say, answered the doctor.

And then they have children, said Kempler. Of course, it's natural, I'll explain that more fully the day after tomorrow. Meantime, think of what I've said.

It came to him, the next day, that he should have asked the doctor if he'd been to a psychiatrist when he was fifteen. Otherwise he was probably a liar. Kempler was learning. It didn't do to trust anyone at all. Though he didn't have much choice now. The Word was out. Teachers and parents, and sisters and brothers, and neighbours and the other casual adult acquaintances of his life let up on their normal, customary backhandings. Even a whole week had gone by without been slapped in school.

Quiet, studious, introspective Kempler had suddenly acquired a reputation for violence. Against adults. And the girl in the library, once so prim, prissy, proper and commanding, showed deference, and noted the titles of the books. Kempler didn't notice it. He went home, put one book in the garden bush as usual, rang the bell and went in.

Is that any good? his mother asked taking the book out of his hands and examining it. Oh! that's nice, she said, they made a musical out of that.

When the coast was clear he retrieved the other and smuggled it into the safety of his father's Sunday suit, open and safe under the trousers folded over the hanger.

So, the doctor asked, what do you think of Sally Bowles? She's a bitch like the rest but I like the writer. The doctor grabbed a pen and scribbled furiously, looked up and asked: 'And what do you think of Blake?'

'Oh the BITCH,' said Kempler.

'WHAT!'

But Kempler knew he'd already said too much.

'They're all spying on you, is that it?' asked the doctor. 'It's persecuting you.'

Kempler stared past him. Say something. He did: Even if they weren't spying and cunnying all the time I still wouldn't like them.

Then the doctor hunched over the desk, joined his hands and began explaining, psychologically and physically, patiently and expertly, about men and women.

It didn't take away the sensed, imaged odour of it all, nor the undignified incongruity of the ritual. But it was good to have the whole mess verified. He hadn't erred in piecing together the schoolboys' rumours and the occasional observations of adult behaviour in its shy or bellowing amorous temper.

Doesn't it hurt them, really, asked Kempler. That was the wrong perspective, answered the doctor after a pause to scribble, on a very complicated, highly complicated, question. But he would find his nature assimilating, osmosifying, sensing, the answer. Words wouldn't do at this primitive stage of understanding. It would become natural later. You understand? The doctor smiled. 'Time is the mercy of eternity' he said, quoting Blake with a smile, (aren't we just great buddies, really. Wink).

Walking home with Michael he told him. It's all true. They examined the men and women passing by on the street. He has to climb up on her can you imagine, oh God. Their bellies were so fat they'd never make contact. But they must have. That face, face to face with that face. You'd have to close your eyes; lust would have been long chastened away. Why then fabricate love? Where do you put your elbows? How do you locate if she doesn't guide? Could you slip into a mistake? And then you start jumping up and down.

I'm going to be a priest, said Michael. That solved it for him. But Kempler liked to shimmy-up trees and he knew he wouldn't be able to do that when he grew up. But to do that with them! Really. And then you'd have to look at their faces afterwards, look into their eyes. And they'd know. They'd get their own back. They'd never let you away with it. They'd make you pay, somehow.

Then something passed across his mind and he saw a way out. He'd tell it to the doctor and that'd be the end of it; and the end of the sessions too. OH NO, DON'T. String the doctor along. Wait. This is very secret. Don't tell anyone. This, above all, you must not tell anyone. No one. Not even Michael. Just wait. Wait. Get it together in your head, it'll come soon. Try harder to suffer the idiots, lay down the scent. Be a normal little boy. Just stay by yourself. Reading is best anyway.

He picked out a man and asked him. Ten after six. Oh God! Three more hours to kill. At least. Better not go back before ten. They'd be a little merry on shandies and gin and try to cuddle. At least the men don't do that. Kempler made a mark. He'd watch to see if they did it to little girls.

A young girl of his own age passed by. She was thin and bony and walked oddly in high-heeled shoes strapped above her ankles by narrow bands. He watched her. She cocked and raised her head, looking away. Kempler laughed, scornfully. Geraway yer little pup, she said, offended.

He was passing another church. The Carmelites owned this one so he couldn't go in. It was always crowded with them. Kempler had never liked them, but he'd never thought that was wrong, or unnatural. It was encouraged, really. Now he was being encouraged to like them, but he couldn't. He hadn't learned. And now they were telling him that was wrong. They were right. Let them.

'To be prudish it is necessary to be guilty. Some forgotten, hidden, perverted lust lies in the action of every prude.'

Kempler knew this from instinct.

'And violence, physical or otherwise, is the reaction of the prude when an act, a word, or strange unusual behaviour threatens to brush aside the scab and expose the perverted lust. They didn't beat and torment, really, for the sake of it. Not all of them anyway. They were trying, forever trying, to bury the unburiable nature of man. Even the most violent of their symptoms, their most fervent — albeit vicarious — protests of the holiness of their causes, cruelly, unconsciously, reflected and magnified the hidden, undying lust growing stronger and more diseased in its airless cavern, squirming ever more violently for release.'

The doctor smiled, to reassure. Adults are very dangerous to deal with. Don't argue with them. In your childish innocence you may say the obvious. And the result of that might scar you for life. And your behaviour and oddity of speech, like mine, is more than a strange statement to them. It is a threat. It tells them you have not been culled by the same received ideas, that you might not know the respect their emblems and words demand. You might laugh at the wrong time. When I say be good I mean be careful. Wink. See you day after tomorrow. Alright.

So, they were right. He knew he was a threat. Fifty pence and say a Rosary. They were being reasonable. To have him in the house that night would invite the obvious to be spoken. And the uproar would need the great male violence of his father to suppress it. The streets were the only answer. No relative could be asked to guard the strange boy who attended one of those Doctors. His problems must be infectious 'cos he just couldn't have got it, by example or by blood, from any of them. They were uproariously sane. That's the truth of the matter, thought Kempler. And he was quietly mad.

A Friday night queue stood at the first cinema. Kempler passed on. Queueing made him feel uneasy. I suppose, he thought, that's another sign. He was happy alone, quite happy. Yet the courting couples, the groups, instead of augmenting his aloneness, seemed to challenge it. Their presence as good as spoke: You are odd, odd, odd. You are alone.

And the problem was girls. It had been quite manly, once, to have a little boy's abhorrence for girls. Now it was quite unmanly. There was no reason not to let Michael out to accompany him; except that reason. Slowly the Word had gone around; the answer had been surmised, been sensed, by their instincts. But what was wrong about not liking women. Didn't they know there was something *unmanly*, effete, something almost unclean about them; some beast-like cunning in their behaviour, some challenge in their superficiality of manners that his nature forbade him to recognise. It made his nature recoil, shudder, turn away. And the cloak of their gentleness, their tenderness, their vulnerability, often parted to expose a sodden, treacherous, animal vileness. Why his nature, his presence, his contented solitude with himself was instinctively sensed by them and instinctively, deeply resented and hated, he could not know. What role was he supposed to play? And what possible threat could he be to them? Somewhere, perhaps, there were some who wouldn't resent him. Some, perhaps, who would not act the ritual of female to male, nor feel spurned by his lack of understanding of this strange ritual. But he had not seen nor heard of any like that anywhere. Not in movies, T.V., not even in books. And certainly not from his mother, aunties, sisters or the girls in the neighbourhood. *They* all seemed to believe that violence would 'cure' him. And if they were not old enough to administer it themselves, they shamelessly and ruthlessly spurred males to administer it for them. Some unspoken, some seemingly unspeakable promise would be passed; some unknown, unknowable secret shared. But however the brutality of the violence fell, it fell in the face of their total indifference to the fate of their victim, and in the total abeyance of their vaunted virtues of gentleness, pity, softheartedness. They were then cold and callous; and showed no sign of the depressed reluctance that blushed, sometimes, across the face of the performing male.

Kempler passed by four cinemas before he found one without a waiting queue. It was an old movie. The main character, always indecisive and undefined, and always wearing a black, leather jacket, was uneducated and mostly inarticulate; a grown-up child and a symbol of his generation. His helplessness, and his helpless bouts of anger, seemed to attract the solicitude and understanding, the mothering and love, of the female characters. And Kempler, forgetting how young the evening was, wandered out of the cinema to ponder the sentiment of the film.

He didn't ponder it. He dismissed it as he realised why he had left. The movie was childishly distracting him from facing his own situation, from articulating it to himself as he walked the streets, ostensibly waiting for ten o'clock.

OH GOD. GOD. He fingered the beads in his pocket. Why was peace so hard to find; and God so easy to please. A few prayers, Church on Sunday, confession now and then, the Act of Contrition. Paradise in return when death came. Perhaps tomorrow, or the next minute, or years and years away. It was easy to love this God. Too easy. It was transparent. Another lie, another diversion insinuated into a child's open, believing mind to push him down the road, struggling, bound and gagged with the other lies and deceits, the other pattern of received thought imprisoning him in a mental cage to stunt him into being a replica of themselves. Pruned by their lies and beliefs to grow in a manner pleasing to them, but tormenting to his nature. And he had never doubted but that they were right. He had believed adults, believed all. His mind had either to wither and die, or go mad, in the cloistered conformity of their sodden, hidden, perverted lusts growing stronger and more vicious in their stinking caverns of unspoken rules, unquestionable values, unmentionable taboos.

Kempler walked to the gutter and dropped the beads into the

sewer. Perhaps it would be better never to go home again. To run away, to find some niche where he could grow and develop, unmolested by the violence of their deeds and beliefs.

He bumped into a woman. Automatically, naturally, he smiled and said sorry. She seemed relieved too and smiled back, answering his sorry with her own. He smiled again. He laughed. The flood of relaxation, of casualness, seemed to have been always there, and not just there, not just a part of him, but himself, his nature. It was the most, most natural feeling he had ever known. It was totally his nature, his element. He was discovering who he was. He was his own child. He knew his virtues and his faults. He was his own man. And he knew now he would grow, by his own rules, and where he would find his happiness; the intense, concentrated, smileless happiness of mirthful insanity.

It would require silent, gentle cunning. But not much. Whatever the qualities of society or of his family, each lived by accepted rules, and each lacked Kempler's now flowering amorality. Society had hung its scales of justice on a cross. The post was success; the spar society's morality. At those co-ordinates an individual's worth lay. And now in Kempler's mind it lay crucified, ready to be speared, with impunity by anyone ruthless enough to exploit mankind's crucifying values. And that ability was freedom's handmaiden. Kempler's favourite and only pastime, his fiendish delight, was his devotion to solitary study. That, he knew, would invincibly lead to unassailable freedom: a licentiousness sedately governed by gentle discretion, by polite, smiling secretiveness.

'Do you vank,' he asked, just like that without any attempt to hide his accent. 'Do you vank?'

And his doctor-confidence seemed to flee for a moment; but only a moment.

'You mean masturbate?' Innocent, wide-eyed, running for time.

'Ah yes.' He smiled, 'My Irish colleagues tell me that is the Gaelic word for birth-control.'

A laugh; and an admittance.

'And vat, what do you think of then?' Moments of silence. 'Please tell me.'

'I rage,' said Kempler, 'only rage.'

'At them?'

'At everyone.'

'Do you know the difference between sadism and aggression?'

'One gives the doer pleasure, the other gives . . .' He was lost.

'Success?'
'I don't know.'
'Pleasure?'
'They'd murder you in my school, doctor.'
'My job is not nice, then? Pulling off scabs.' Kempler froze.
'Proud flesh. That's the term for skin crusted over a wound.'
'Yes. I know. I am a doctor.'

And so it went on, as if honesty were enough to banish all the spectres from a mind that did not belong to him, to Kempler. A mind that was never under his control, but a mind that viciously, invincibly dominated him. There was no conflict there, not anymore, only different grades of surrender, conditional or absolute. Unknown forces, unshaped by him, patrolled and dictated in the mind that had once been a pasture, then a battlefield, now a wasteland treacherous with live munitions, traps, and booby-trapped remnants of forgotten, never seen, corpses; and poisoned rations marked inspected and safe. And, for want of other food, from lack of guidance, daily consumed by the fog-blinded, bewildered, shell-shocked child stumbling towards the safety of adulthood where he might arrive undamaged, or arrive forever crippled.

The oddity in his speech remained and lisped strangely with his strange hearing. His speech sounded correct to his hearing. They sounded odd, acoustically, then intellectually. And his parents said no to drugs, as fervently as Jehovah Witnesses recoil at surgery. Mental ill-health was there to be suffered, by the Will of God, otherwise it wouldn't be there. No one was to blame. Offer it up as a sacrifice to God. Slaughter a lamb. Transubstantiate suffering into virtue. Oh yes; they lived off flesh and blood.

Kempler smiled. Perhaps the doctor would be interested to hear that Goethe was a vegetarian, but looked robust and healthy when Kempler met him leaving the church. And God, when Kempler told him, only remarked that His son was also a storyteller. BUT NO! NO! DON'T OVERDO IT. Just get some books from the library-spy, hide them as ever, and wait for one of the doctor's baited questions. Swallow it, whole, then squirm, rant. Sneer madly at Helen, mutter a contorted, illogical comparison to Bowles. Declare rebellion on woman's brevetted rank — as if this were a vanity unique and exclusive to them. Pollute Blake, demand your sovereignty: 'Spectre of Me! Mad Fiend! in clouds of blood and ruined childhood roll'd — I here proclaim thee as my own — My Self-Hood! Satan! arm'd in gold.'

Softly, without struggle, the doctor would 'cure' him in a month.

Kempler walked towards the docks. At the last bridge before the ships' berthing quays he saw a round-shouldered, stooped youngman leaning over the parapet and gazing down, dreamlike at the languorously flowing water. Kempler stood beside him. The youngman turned, cautiously, to look at him. Kempler smiled. The youngman returned to gazing at the water. Kempler waited. 'Would you like to go for a walk?' the youngman asked without looking up. 'Yes. Of course.' replied Kempler.

They walked up the other side of the quay without speaking, towards the city's main bridge. From there they saw the commotion outside the university gates. Bob didn't want to go, he wanted to avoid the police, but Kempler insisted. And stupidly Bob became nervous and fretful as they approached the crowds. And this warranted fear, Kempler knew, bundled Bob more deeply into his mercy, into that commodity which was just one more instrument of expediency. Yet beautifully, irreproachably, named.

They brushed past the stragglers at the fringe of the crowd, then edged their way to the university gates where the police had formed a line to separate the opposing groups. Placards waved and bobbed in the air, for and against the Motion being debated far inside the sheltered university: The Right to Abortion.

The slogans on the placards were no more intelligible. 'The Right to Life' from one side, 'The Right to our own Bodies' from the other. Gleefully, Kempler collected opposing emblems and badges before giving in to Bob's entreaties and hurrying back down the street to the main bridge. They turned to walk towards the Law Courts and Bob's apartment, while Kempler selected episodes from his visits to the doctor for Bob's amusement. 'God as a transparent lie?' asked Bob, 'Is that a pun?' Oh God, thought Kempler, he's no better than the crowd at the university. No, he didn't know what enantiosis meant. Couldn't see the trees for the forest. Oh yes, I see. Then: You'll have to explain what osmosifying means I'm afraid. Oh, I see, and a note of unease, of suspicion, creeping into Bob's voice. Kempler continued. 'Oh good God no.' said Bob, 'Of course it doesn't hurt them.' Kempler eyed him, and allowed him to see that he was being eyed. 'How do *you* know?' he asked, finally, with all the bluntness and cruelty he could insinuate.

'I think, really, that that ought to be perfectly obvious.'

No more was said. They walked quietly on. Police cars and troop tenders became more numerous as they neared the vicinity of the Law

Courts. Kempler watched the dour-faced troops staring out of the back of the tenders. They looked fit, well-fed, healthy, sulkily confident. And very dangerous. And they seemed to enjoy that, patrolling in the inner heart of a city already impounded with so many grim, rank, military barracks studded about it like so many nails in a coffin.

Occasionally a civilian car with troops in mufti cruised by. One could tell them by their fit, well-fed, confident faces and their ever alert eyes. The permanency of their presence on the streets was plain; and an eternity away from the world of debating societies.

Kempler tried to turn down onto a street leading away from the quays. Bob stopped him in time, and they stood to watch another group with yet more placards demonstrating outside a non-Catholic institution for the poor. 'No soupers here' the placards read, 'No Proselytising here.' And the indisputably Catholic police trying to keep order looked abashed and ashamed, as if they had been demoted to schoolwardens. A stone's throw away, on the other side of the quays, stood a famous church most renowned, once, for the peal of its bells to proclaim to the citizens that their priests were destitute and hungry.

This, indeed, was the area of extremes, and the area where the unnameable were brought to trial in screaming convoys of troop tenders, squad cars, black marias, outriders, troop tenders, squad cars and, stringing along at the back, an ominous ambulance. And, at odd times of the day and night, the same convoys screeched again out of the area in a blaze of sirens, racing away to the incongruously rural, bucolic prisons.

Nervously, Bob shook his head: no, he didn't know the unnameable were, to themselves, the word enomoty. He didn't want to know.

They walked on, as the wail of the sirens faded. They passed a troop of soldiers guarding the entrance to the Four Courts. The troops stood in two spaced lines of every other one cradling his machine-pistol towards the ground, every other one cradling his towards the sky. They looked almost casual in their black, nailed boots and their warm, comfortable looking, military sweaters, their well-pressed, heavy trousers smartly tucked into polished gaiters. And from them came a sullen, menacing lethargy; and the potent smack of the grim realities shadowing the ghost of a resumed, but unproclaimed, civil war.

Bob looked very frightened. 'Of course,' Kempler said to reassure him, 'this doesn't happen in the suburbs.'

'I should think not' Bob said.

'Does it frighten you?' Kempler asked. 'Yes it does and I see it almost every day.' Bob snapped, angered. Kempler was puzzled. 'But why? They won't harm you.'

'Yes. But it still frightens me. For God's sake, that's its purpose.'

They hurried on, past another barracks, and down some littered bedsitter-streets. Bob's bedsitter was clean and well-ordered, warm and inviting. When they entered the tension broke and they fell upon the bed laughing. Kempler pulled the emblems from his pockets and stuck them on the wall over the bed. 'The Right to Life' and 'The Right to our own Bodies'. They were crude and childish.

'Which one would a foetus wear, I wonder?' asked Kempler.

'Neither' said Bob, then laughed. 'He'd ask: "What's left?".'

So Bob wasn't so poor at puns after all. Not so dim. And wise enough to accept Kempler's terms and give in to his blackmail. Bob knew, by the vocabulary, by the laugh, by the perpetually indifferent, calm eyes and the stories of the visits to the doctor, that Kempler was mad, and very, very dangerous. He was glad to pay and see him leave; and lamely forego the always unending hope for sympathy, understanding, acceptance. Then he cursed himself, like all fools, knowing he couldn't have been tricked by a mere boy if he hadn't wanted to be; hadn't wanted to pay, in this way, for some lurking, hidden, well-learned and fully accepted, sense of guilt.

Kempler knew that guilt, and expertly played on it. Just one more proof of his nimble madness. Bob sighed an extra sigh of relief.

Kempler was calm, composed, and humble as he walked down the streets. Only in the back of his head did his friends' uproarious quips and laughter scamper, highly intelligently, with each other; and scorn, with satanic glee, the innate cowardice of the much-too-sane. For they, the much-too-sane have lost their minds. They have become the strong, proud, articulate sheep of morality and conformity. Well softened, well frightened, and ripe for the Kemplers. And so his scampering friends told him. Touch here, brush there, shoo the sheep to the exciting fringe of their morality, their conformity, or wherever you wish to have them go. Conduct them there by their own vanities of sympathy, anger, empathy, compassion, justice. Any of the beautiful, irreproachably named instruments which come readily to hand to orchestrate them into their state of grace; lay them vulnerable then to the fear of the fall from grace, falling foul of what you have taught them to adore. And so, thought Kempler, they come ready-harnessed, thank God.

Abruptly he stopped. His scampering friends disappeared. Painted in a scrawl of the quay wall the coldless, warmless reality read: Ask your police army. 1979 makes 1984 look like 1966.

Kempler read it again. But what was the significance of 1966? Was that the . . . . .

A civilian-military car slowed to a stop beside him and its occupants serenely eyed him, then the slogan, then Kempler again. He stared back, his endlessly calm, alert eyes searching every facet of the car. Just forward of the gear lever he caught a glimpse of the fat, perforated barrel of the machinegun. The car slowly moved, almost lingered, then cruised smoothly and silently, ominously, away.

Kempler walked on, mindlessly, physically, alone.

The Anniversary, of course. The innocuous, painless, fiftieth Anniversary. But did Time mock History; or History Time? Or were they playing dice with each other?

He passed the line of troops again, still standing in their gung-ho, sheriff's deputies postures. He eyed them enviously, and allowed his envy to show on his face. They reacted as he knew they must: grown men proud to be the envy of a little boy. God, he thought, Oh God, I could be a successful Richard of Gloucester with such infantry.

And Kempler's deranged mind deformed the word to the infancy of its sounds. He understood the doctor; and understood that the doctor knew he understood. They would play with it at the next session. Onomatopoeia. And his lisping, mis-pronouncing tongue against the doctor's foreign, meticulous enunciation of English must fuse them together as allies against the glib, plaintive, jappering mouths of the mindlessly sane.

The marked police car screeched to a halt ten yards ahead. Kempler froze. The lone policeman jumped from the car, its door hanging wide across the path and the blue rooflight flashing in sweeps around the silent street. He approached, broad and massive, in rapid, measured, echoing steps. Kempler stood, horrified, bereft of his scampering friends' solitude and security.

A hand fell firmly on his shoulder, and Kempler turned to see the two civilian-dressed police. And saw, immediately, the tactic; and the calculated lethalness of his enemy. Only fear had saved him from turning, in the first rush of panic, and fleeing into their arms in a blatant scab of guilt.

He answered their questions truthfully, while the uniformed policeman stood and watched. The oddity of his voice puzzled them. That showed. They became a little cautious. A touch of deference shadowed their questions. Then they were satisfied, and quite reasonable, too. That showed. Only Kempler didn't have any identification. It was so unfortunate we weren't obliged to carry identity cards, hm? the matter would be settled in minutes, wouldn't it, hmm? it was such a reasonable solution, wasn't it?

Kempler's mind raced blindly to play the child for them, to concur with eagerness and vigour, to flash a sign of envious flattery, to wield any expediency and disarm these menacing, untrustable enemies.

'Everyone could be tatooed at birth and you could carry books like telephone directories.'

They didn't laugh. They didn't say a word in response. They stared hard at him, and the threat of great, imminent violence hung in their stance. The Doctor's words pounded in Kempler's empty, terrified mind. He had laughed at the wrong time.

'But you'll soon have fingerprint transmitters, won't you, like teevee, and the computers will identify them all.'

It did. They relaxed. No scab of prudery had been touched. The strange little fellow was only trying to be a big policeman.

'C'm'on, Mr. Kempler,' said the uniformed one, 'We'll drive you home.'

Another trick? Another test? A free joyride in a squadcar. For nothing?

'We'll explain it to your Dad. Don't worry' the uniformed one said.

'It's the neighbours, Sir. He'll be thinking of them. When you've gone. And we live in a good street, Sir.'

It worked immediately. The appropriate values had been mirrored and the opiate blinded them. And the bright little animal in his head instinctively noted another technique for dealing with these . . . .

Kempler was lost. For a word. As mute as a bright little animal performing tricks in a laboratory, observing the rulers of his universe. And their requirements. His life depended on it. But he couldn't name it. Not yet. Only accept their guidance. Follow the paths where they have laid the rewards. Put down your head and don't look up. They're always watching. If they catch you watching them they'll be very interested in you. You'll get picked up and examined in detail. Are you a nut or somethin'?

'Get to hell outa here.' The uniformed one stood aside and let him pass. Minutes later he heard the car pass. He pretended to be lost in thought.

The streets became empty of note as he walked the streets; streets after streets passed without alerting any response as his blank, emptying mind, working in secret, gave way to the tremors of shock.

He passed his own house without wanting to go in. He sat against a garden wall and closed his eyes. Copper blue, barium green, sodium yellow, diamond white. Mathesis, the doctor said, you must develop mathesis. Learn to control yourself, inside your head. Name your thoughts, pursue them to the end of your understanding, then play dice with them. That way you might get lucky. If the sadist is pleased by pleasing the masochist by ignoring him what's wrong with that? They're both abnormal. Men and women, mankind, humanity? Masochists please each other by ignoring each other. Only sadists fight. That's aggression? But it pleases each. What a happy world. Don't look up. If this isn't dice what's the name of the game? The harmony of the spheres is a soulless, silent wail.

Kempler pondered, like an ancient thinker. Imagine an underwater appletree. It cannot exist except in your imagination, where it now exists, newly created. And the water? Where does it exist? The doctor proudly raised his head and winked. If what does exist and what does not exist, exist comfortably in your head, where are all the answers? In your imagination? Waiting for questions?

The doctor smiled. Mathesis. We're not rats in a box. We do as we desire. We're not tricked with bread. We know exactly what we're getting and why.

Kempler looked up, thinking why, staring past Carmel. His eyes blinked. She was from the next terrace, as old as Kempler and as skinny. But her hips had already spread and she looked awkwardly formed.

'What's wrong with you?' she asked.

Kempler focused on her instantly. 'Nothing. What's wrong with you?'

She seemed to sigh a little as she put her hands behind her and rested on the wall. 'They sent me down to the shops to get a message,' she said, 'I didn't think there'd be anybody out.'

It was of no concern to Kempler and he ignored her. But in the silence of the street and the dimming of the night, an ancient tableau formed of lovers in trist.

'They say you're a bit mad, you know.' she said. It was a normal, girlish, opening to courtship. She looked down the street, away from him, unconcerned for the answer except for the jangle of vulnerability in her voice.

'Prove to me you don't exist.' he said.

'How?'

'Don't touch me.'
'I don't want to!' she said, immediately defensive.
'Then prove to me you do exist.'
She hesitated, more defensive, more plainly vulnerable. 'How?' she asked, a little frightened that her own instincts were trapping her, not sure that she really wanted the trap to close. Her eyes, uneasy, caught his; and asked for a cue she might understand.
'Do something you don't want to do.'
She surmised; and relaxed. Surmised naturally and wrongly. This she could understand. They all wanted that. But Kempler knew that too. He was thinking of the doctor, and he didn't want to be a doctor's little animal forever, a source for notes scribbled on a page. He wanted to press the correct lever and get out of their clutches before it was too late. Getting out of the doctor's was only the first. Then came the emblems, quay walls, and debating worlds. For a start he needed the camouflage of normality.
'I'll help you get the messages.'
Her face was still airy and distantly indifferent as she pushed off the wall.
'Alright.'
It was tactical whether he should try to hold her hand or not. He tried. She brushed it away, bashful, and laughed a little. It brought a little charm to the rebuttal. He smiled.
'Is it true,' she asked, holding her head high in her odd walk, 'that you don't talk normal 'cos you used to speak something foreign?'
It was so dumb, idiotic, pathetic, so much of everything he abhorred that he felt he had panicked into grabbing the wrong contingency. She wasn't even a contingency now, just a bloody burden.
'NO,' he whispered, angered. 'NO!' Then he reached and took her hand and held it firmly. She was quite relaxed. The bloody bitch just didn't understand.
'Carmel,' he said, 'Carya Sulcata.'
She was pleased. She beamed, radiantly. 'That's lovely,' she said. 'What does it mean?'
'It's a baby's name' he lied.
'OH!' And she laughed a little and bowed her head in her funny walk.
Why tell her. It was the name of a species of tree; one that he liked to shimmy-up, occasionally. The joke would be lost on her. That was obvious. Better let her bow her head and surmise; wrongly again.

Twice they passed his house, then finally to hers with the messages. They're even too dumb to shop properly, but he'd known that a long time and was no longer surprised by it.

'I can't let you come into the passage' she said.

OH GOD, GOD. To stop himself from laughing he turned and looked up at the sky. GOD! But to Carmel it was a boy's courting gesture and she was happy to take the groceries piled into her arms and stand defenceless, happy and expectant, the onus on Kempler leaving her to play her girlish role, blamelessly.

He tried to look at her eyes then bowed his head and looked at the ground. OH GOD! GOD! If he laughed now all would be lost. BUT GOD! Yet he laughed. She laughed too, following the guide. Then he turned away and said goodnight. Oh it was delightful in the back of his head. If she knew! She thinks I want to bob her haw-haw-haw. To bob her. Credits flashed on the screen before the evening's movie. Wardrobe director: Jesus Patrick Gonzales. Oh God. To bob her. O all the world to nothing.

He was still smiling as he glanced up at his mother waiting at the door. There was a change in her. She began to fuss over him, to gently defer to him, while his father was treated as of second rank. For the first time in his life Kempler thought that was wrong. He was ushered into the parlour, and presented, as a young man, to the few remaining party guests. His father, in his proper place, shook his Kulak head. And the manner spoke: it's wonderful what the doctors can do nowadays.

No hint of any possible admonition touched any word or gesture or look. All the rows, the quarrels, the senseless punishments, all the snot and tears of childhood might never have existed. He had, accidentally, but like a bright little animal, pushed the correct lever in the box of their values.

Then he knew. Twice past the windows holding a young girl's hand. He had shown his movements to the flock; and they were pleasing. They knew, now, he was about to hatch into adulthood. He was not different, after all. The species of family was saved, the parents sensing they were shortly to become surplus to the species. These people were animals! They deferred only from weakness, from an assumed sense of growing inferiority, from an assumed sense of growing, of being, worthless. What questions could you expect from these grown-up children, these self-styled adults? When they ask who is God they are asking who is the murderer. Who is the Genocide. That is all life is to them: a passage to death festooned with senseless emblems, death-robbed values.

If this wasn't dice with a loaded die what was it? And they were happy so long as the die kept rolling. It had to be kept rolling. At all costs, at all costs, the dice had to be kept rolling. They didn't want it to stop! Dumb animals in a box doing exactly what they wanted to do. And somehow knowing why. What imaginary ocean did they share together? What was the sum of their being, their times, their histories. Was this an interlude of chance, that we may know no more, and be less, than we may imagine? But they knew life was a lottery. The Winner could have no more than the crowd's sum. And that can only be nothing when the crowd has disappeared, has gone, forever. Nothingness has parts, and their sum is nothing. Somewhere in nothingness we exist as a probability. It is the lottery to exist by probability. And nowherelse as something else. Otherwise we imagine ourselves. O all the world to nothing.

Kempler assumed the demeanour expected. To play this game well you had to forget you were merely playing a mindless game. And he knew his role. The glee shrieked in the back of his head. It had to be said again, for another demoniac laugh. Throw the dice. He knew his role.

For the present he had only to assume a growing fondness for Carya Sulcata. And so long as the bitch remained stupid and trapped in the maze of her role he would bear with her, smilingly but mirthlessly, and encourage her. Pretend to take them all all seriously.

Courteously he bade goodnight to all. On the stairs, as a gesture to humanity, he chased the cat. He chased it 'cos it ran and it too ran 'cos he chased it.

Alone, in the silence of the landing, he paused and looked back down the stairs he had ascended. He couldn't go back down, to ask for a scone or something. No. Such childish things could not be done anymore. Not for many, many years. Not until this struggle across the threshold of adulthood had been mastered, if ever it were mastered. Until then, he had no time for childish things. But in sleep he would dream. Dream, in the protection of adulthood, the dreams children know, before they lose their minds to sanity.

Fixing

THE UNIVERSITY STANDS OPEN, unsheltered and unencumbered by perimeter walls, at one end of the Grindelallee. Opposite it, demurely, stands the library. Inside, in peace, in the sanctity of study, pages are thumbed, notes scribbled, sentences underlined; and thoughts are learned. And your lame, limping mind is caressed by the splashing vigour of reading, learning, by the wonders so arbitrarily denied to, and missed by, so many.

As you walk from there to Dammtor railway station the lines of track along the embankment are hidden from view. Bushes, scrub, and a haphazard line of trees soothe the road's edge. It's a very beautiful stroll, from Grindelallee to Dammtor. Very beautiful. I wish I might go back again. If ever I live again, I will go back. Perhaps I will live again.

A junky never tells it the way it is. Words bounce, meaningless, in his mouth. That's part of the junk. Sometimes, maybe, a freak combination illuminates a nubile insight and the nymph of meaning is had, pulsating, and truth ejaculates. I would sell my soul for junk's heaven. I would look eternity in the face, and turn away and give my soul for junk. I need nobody, nothing, but. Why should I?

That's the logic and speech of a junky's reasoning. Coming down, going cold, has been told only one way: pain, vomit, horror. No mention of the heaven, the paradise on earth, when you know you're down and safe. Whole. You've survived, one out of a lucky few, a nightmare flight, a catastrophe, a human tragedy. But yet, in the terminal's hospital, when you're warm again, and washed of the fear, and life is in your mouth tasting babynew and delightful, relieved, you start talking of the flight, the tremors, the terrifying sickness of the ragged sheets of broken nerves hitting your brain; of the broken, human debris you had to wade through. And you think you've learned something, that you're a better person for the experience. It was unique. And deep down you're glad for it. Yeah. Deep down you're glad.

But I've some pulsating news for you. You're still high on your junk. And you're going to die. You will never feel the gates of paradise roll open as the wheels skim, turn, grip, then roll you safely home. And you're never going to live again, and your presence will not haunt the living. But then, perhaps you've never lived. Listen.

Ralph was his name. Peter Ralph. It was assumed. He was seventy, tall, thin, and not quite broken. But not whole. There was a tenseness in him. A coiled, twisted spring wound to a hard bobbin of determination. Yet still not whole, not himself. The effort of will filled in the missing bits, and added to the tension of stretched nerves firmly held; and the subsequent lack of control, an inability, to be peaceful, calm, quiet, relaxed. To sit and read, casually; or study, understand, absorb, as a natural act. It was an immensity requiring a rigidly applied act of will. It was habit, then, to him. He seemed to have forgotten the effort it required to walk through the daylight. But I had watched him, and I was sure I knew. All of his self-discipline was as useful as my slothfulness. And it served the same purpose: to cover the missing bits. But its mere presence, so unnatural, so assumed, so immovable, poisoned the intention before it became an act. His determination forced him to act his intention naturally. And so it would be. And so the merest rein of effort poisoned itself. Take away the habit, the effort of will, the determination; and he would have exploded into broken, jangling pieces of human debris.

He lived across the hall from me in the basement of a tenement slum. I lay in my room most days. There was nothing else to do. I was already past saving then, except to myself. Occasionally, for a moment in some dream, I would see salvation; see my broken-down mind healthy and youthful again. Then the vision would pass and it wouldn't matter. Once a week I buried my head in the collar of my overcoat, shuffled stealthily to the doctor's. Then I'd draw my paper and then I'd draw my welfare money, silently. With a little care they don't notice you. Shuffle, ignore eyes, scribble your name. Get out of there and back to the cold safety of the room. Stare at the ceiling. The days pass. You wash when the grime begins to itch too much, and you wash the body with disdain. There's only the purpose of purposelessness. You don't want to know, to tell the truth or to lie, to eat or not eat, and it's not tragic or comic. It is. You are. That's enough. Just a retired animal, stripped of instincts, lying down to stare indifferently at the world. At that time I had never tasted alcohol, nor taken anything stronger than a vitamin pill. But what had passed was present. You disappear when you examine yourself. There's nothing there in the shadow, the reflection. You are there and time moves. Then you have changed place without moving. That's how you become a reflection, that's how you part from you. Once, maybe, you dream, and you're whole again for an instant. For a moment you are not a covered, washed, fully-operational but fully-helpless, savage. Savage, because so much of what is known is not known by you; so much of what you know is black magic to you. And so you lie on the dirty bed and stare at the ceiling, while your mind moves from place to place and time to time, and the wondering savage stares helplessly at the theatre.

Sometimes appetite stirs and you know you must creep out past the world, get some food. You wait for the darkness of night, when the jungle streets are safe. Then you steal to the all-night store, pluck some foods off the dead shelves, silently pay, and return along the dark streets. Be nimble; or voices might shriek from one human to another; or ask you something. And you stand terrified of the speaking cadaver, knowing some sounds will communicate with it, some inflections in their chants give rhythm meaning, evoke a response. Their rituals are your ordeals. The dread swallows your appetite, separates your existence as you stand apart and sense the encounter of savage to savage in the darkening twilight before consciousness. Even when you articulate the mumbles and groans correctly they seem to sense an animal not of their herd. They move with eyes, with odd movements of the face, with changes in their stance, and scout you, suspiciously. Then you quickly bow the gestures of submission with an appropriate sound, an appropriate apologizing crouch. Then you retreat, you must, or the panic will suffocate you.

That's how I met Ralph. Coming back, treading silently and peacefully, I found his hulk stumbling at the bottom of the stairs. He wore sunshades, day and night, indoors and out, and now he stopped pawing his hands back and forth across the wall. The light was already on. I had no retreat. I had to get past to my room. Ralph started to feel, gently, cautiously, around him, his arms going out further and further. Then he'd step and search the air again. I gauged his movements until I had a corridor wide enough to slip through. So long as we passed, unchallenged by pleasantries or shadows, the ethos would be preserved. So long as we both believed the other didn't exist, the easier it seemed to exist.

'I'm trying to cook, goddamn,' he said, 'And the heat went off.'

I saw the coin in his open palm, reached for it, shoved it into the meter and cranked the lever. The coin dropped away, the noise dimly, just dimly, perceptible. The thought passed my mind that the meter must be nearly full.

'I'm near blind.' But I had moved and he was peering towards the wrong place. He started to guide himself by the wall into his own room.

'Well, do what you want. I've met them all.'

I waited for him to close his door. He didn't. I was offended. I liked the slum ethos of nobody knowing, acknowledging, anyone else. I wanted to keep it. Intact.

'That's not worth stealing.' He shouted from inside his room. I looked at the meter. Someday. Perhaps. In desperation. I'd never stolen so little before. Yet I might be hungry enough someday. A radio voice came on, East German Radio, and Ralph said, under its cover: 'Best way to go cold is to die.'

A layman would never think of saying that. Only a junky sees coming down as death, hard death, where laymen, the cadavers live. It's a form of death and existence as childhood is to an adult; a state of life, but not really, real life. The eyes haven't fully opened. They're nice, children and laymen, when you're really high. You pat them on the head, in admiration, and with a wondering sense of loss that they do not know this voyage. And they smile back, delighted, not understanding it is a voyage, a journey to a destination, and the smile is its climax, the rest pathos.

I opened the door of my room and went in. My appetite returned. I opened the cans of food. Boiled rice, beetroot, potato salad, tinned fish. I ate from can to can, back and forth, ravenously. When it was finished I still needed to eat, but that was all I'd bought and I couldn't face going back through the streets for more. I was a little high, a little healthy, on the rush of food in my body; opening, closing arteries, breathing audibly, a flush, an aura, across my brain. It subsided a little when I stood up, but I pushed on, still enveloped in the heat of the food. I went across the hall and tapped on Ralph's door. It opened.

'Hello,' I said, breaking the news, 'I live across the hall.' My voice sounded strange and distant. Ralph turned and went back into the room, leaving the door open. I followed and closed the door. In the room he moved surely and easily; almost as if he could see everything. He was cooking over an electric plate. Tomatoes sliced in halves, dipped in the burning oil, crusted, then out onto a plate. Eggs bubbled by breaking the shell, then ducking the shell into the oil. Beautiful. Strips of liver, fistfuls of mushrooms, chipped potatoes, bread with margarine on it. It was mountainous.

The radio still blared on. Poverty in Western Europe, unemployment, strikes, demonstrations.

'Gotta eat,' Ralph said, 'Gotta eat. Bad days ahead. I remember.'

To the lay this would mean an old man watching the cycle of history. To a junky it's literal. You remember the future. You know it, wait for time to move, then experience it. The future is merely the end of the voyage. Meantime you stand quarantined in junk watching the parade of time pass, as a movie. Otherwise you don't move.

My voice cracked again. It'd been so long since I used it that I could listen to myself enunciating and puncturing the words: 'How did you get all of this?'

'All of what?' Ralph asked back, the trivial future already past. 'It's all I got.'

There was no gluttony, just the casual, graceful sweeps, the restful chewing, of a lion eating a horse.

Each time I eat now, in private or in public, each time I sit to eat, I remember, by heart, the manners of Ralph. And the cat-o'-nine-tails scars on his back; and the graceful, courteous enormity of his indifferent, lionish appetite so totally unmarred by touches of greediness or prudery.

Months before the collapse of Germany in 1918 Ralph had been conscripted as a boy soldier. In 1933 he'd been flogged in prison. In '45 he'd been again conscripted. So he got food parcels from an ex-servicemen's organisation, from an organisation for ex-prisoners, from an organisation for the blind. And then he got Welfare. Ralph never wasted a scrap.

Perhaps he saw it only in a blur, perhaps he sensed and heard the silent tremblings of my body and my hands as I ate, but he asked me what hospital I'd been in. I told him.

'Where've you got them?' he asked, 'Head or hands or belly or where?'

I told him. He mumbled something, something about being born. I mumbled something about trying to cure myself and he nodded in sympathy.

'If you can do it, DO IT!' I said.

'I thought you already knew.' He said.

'Please.' I said. I leaned forward, closed my eyes, covered them with the palms of my hands. 'Please.' I said.

I heard him as he went about the room, collecting gear. He muttered under his breath. Then his hand felt around the lower calf of my leg, passed to my ankle, and squeezed out the skin at the side. The needle dipped into the vein, lingered, then reluctantly withdrew. I waited, and wondered about the mind that is each one's fatherland, from hence some of us manage to crawl with the belief that this life, this consciousness, is not the greatest feat of this universe.

I moved; and time stood, to watch. Time stopped, the air turned to velvet, the colours awoke and smiled, the walls around me released their imprisonment, the bricks and paving stones of the city jumbled into a child's toy in a country field, green and lush on a young summer's day. The torment, my lifelong torment, ceased.

It was then that I knew, with pellucid clarity, that I had been a junky from the moment I was conceived. I had been longing, all of my life, for this release. All of my love for my Love, all of my happiness, all of the sweetness, the joy of the welcome, grew and grew. And I closed my eyes in peace, and drowned the remnants of my life in that ocean of happiness.

The wasted years, dormant in their life, finally passed.

I was free of them. All I had ever known, from the hands that guided as the womb released me, to the dozens of other hands that had marshalled my life, to the last, idiotic doctor who told me it was all in my head, a primeval memory, a damaged child still kicking to grow, all released their hold on me and became the twisted, broken limbs of the human debris I had had to wade through.

I moved; and they remained.

Ralph disappeared from his shadow, lost the predominance of his body. There was no going back. Mankind disappeared, severed from its actions, its actions the only definition of the undulating shadows flickering over the field's earth. Then gone. The future is passed. All is gone. It paid no attention to us, a primitive, antiquated species moving forward in negative time.

This is why words bounce meaningless in a junky's mouth. All is explained before he can say a word. Everything has been explained in placid terms of undiscovered quarks, unfound nutrions and the simplistic junk of science founded on The Big Bang or The Big Man. And mankind, examining itself, finds itself already disappeared. Yesterday's nutrions.

That first time the Junk stayed with me for a honeymoon. My body had its fill of food, my brain its fill of junk. I sat in eternity, content. Planets moved and clocks followed and people obeyed the call to eclipse. Good, gentle people; thoughtful, concerned people, did not understand their clean secret was found and told. They continued to move their shadows after the movements of the hypnotising pendulums.

I heard Josie's voice retail the story of a car stopped at a pedestrian's crossing. A young woman, robed and smeared and shining in glamour on the way to her day's production sat, the passenger of an executive of the workplace, and screamed and cried: 'help me! help me!' The driver was slumped over the wheel, jerked by death. And the young woman sobbed and sobbed. Passersby pulled the man back against the seat, loosened the beauty of his necktie from around his throat, unbuttoned the collar of the clean, fresh shirt from against his warm, washed skin. Then they laid him on the road and blew air into his mouth, made his chest heave, pushed it back, filled his lungs again, pushed again, establishing the pneumatism of life. But the meaning was gone, at a pedestrian-crossing, and the crowd stood aghast and humiliated, waiting for the ambulance. They thought life had now become a waste disposal problem.

Ralph was cooking again. Josie had brought more groceries. She took her own junk. She knew how. Ralph only stored it for her. During the midday workbreak, and in the evenings, Josie worked as a whore in the Brennerstrasse. She would lounge against the wall, her fingers moving in the patchpockets of her coat. She always had patchpockets so that she could read a Braille book while she stared at the streets, searching for customers. Then she'd take the customer upstairs to a small room of infinite possibilities where he'd pay for the most trite of things. She'd wash him, gently massage him dry, then bear with him while he suffered the rape of a force he could not control, nor escape.

I understood. Sex was a force whose autonomy I could not tolerate, within me or within the mellowness I had seen darken a girl's eyes as she looked at me. It reproduces not us, but itself. We are its carriers, burdened and oppressed by its demands, never satisfied from it, merely occasionally rested from its yoke, then re-burdened. Sex is a master, but I could not be its contented employee, nor a seeker for another employee whom I could embrace and, together, occasionally shed our burden. Sex is ego junk, but Ralph's junk banished the ego, gave me freedom. A smile for a girl, a smile from a girl, was a smile for the beauty of flowers on our journey deeper into the cosmos. So I felt shamed when I saw the egos shuffle through the darkened jungle ways of procuring a partner and taking, finally, whatever they could get, like I plucked tinned food from the cold shelves of the all-night store, and silently paid.

Josie came to Ralph's every day. So did I. But in between times I no longer lay in my room. I used life. I strolled through the daylight a whole human being. I read in the library, took walks in the park; and one day I found a cat, a real, fourlegged cat, and took him to my room that had shed its emptiness. I named the cat the Blue Nepalese. He was junked on something and seemed flattered. I started to happily-live-life. A freak combination had scored.

I went to the doctor, junked. I went through a series of tests. The doctor congratulated himself. I was cured. No longer a jangling mass of broken purposes and half-formed personalities in need of care and attention; and bolts of electricity. I told the doctor I was junked. He told me I was killing myself. Killing myself! Life at a pedestrian-crossing but I could not understand him. I had been released from a living death, an inadequate animal in a strange, foodless jungle, a hapless creature who could find nothing in life and the doctor said I was killing myself to escape. It was also against the law. So. I never went back to that outwardly civilised man. I had always known that to the outwardly civilised I was basically a waste disposal problem and not so many volts away from the Sing Sing final solution.

My nice doctor had been civilised by studying the mechanics of anatomy with a brain of his own that was black magic to him. He lived in this world too as an inadequate animal, only he suffered no awareness of it. More purposeful in his ignorance, more convinced that he was he and he was right. But his peace was lack of mind; his steadiness, his calm confidence came from being a good, blindly obedient servant of a force he never sought to know.

But I was fixed, everyday. I found a job and every morning I'd stroll along Grindelallee to Dammtor and take the train to Bremer-reihe. There I pulled the seats from used cars, scrubbed their upholstery, washed the floormats, glossed and polished everything inside, replaced the seats, closed the doors, then buffed the bodywork. And everyday I'd hear Otto, the owner, ask customers just to look, the last owner treated it like a baby, it was really brand new. And every evening I returned along Grindelallee with money in my pocket. So with great happiness I set about organising my life. Otto smiled to see me each morning, thought me a smiling, harmless fool happy as only a lunatic could be. But I loved restoring beauty; there could never be slavery in the happiness of fixing me and fixing the also punished, mankind-damaged, harmless cloth and steel. I talked to those cars, treated each one differently, according to its personality. They seemed to need love too. And each morning I smiled back at Otto, and each morning an extra dimension of happiness seemed to glint from his eyes. My eyes fixed his. He thought I loved him as a Saviour, as a peasant his lord. But I loved him as Jesus loved, because I loved all.

Ralph once told me it was the custom of the ancient Romans to fix victims before crucifixion, in the manner of the belated and self-serving kindness of the Christians strangling their victims behind the smoke of the stake. So it made sense of Jesus to pre-empt his father's judgement and tell his fellow-victims that they would be in paradise that day. He knew. He'd taken junk before. And his father has many mansions.

That was where I lived then, each day, at the side of the Grindelallee. And there too, Josie took me into her arms and taught me to take sex as naturally as Ralph ate his food. And we laughed, like baby cubs, each time we copulated. Naked, playful, laughing, we fed each other's joy, and pushed and muzzled and scampered and lay all sorts of ways, and slept. Often, watching us, we could hear the Blue Nepalese purr.

So much is said about cats, but I've searched libraries from end to end without ever finding an explanation for their affinity with addicts. So when the Blue Nepalese disappeared I worried. Normally he waited for me each evening. I came home but he wasn't there. I searched all the corridors and closets right up to the attic. Then I tried Ralph's. But he hadn't heard him all day. I was afraid now, and a little suspicious. Ralph might have casually cooked and ate him. I checked the garbage cans outside for remains, then I told Ralph to hold my dinner while I checked the streets. An hour later I came back, defeated. Ralph normally had a meal cooked for me each evening, but I was too depressed. I went to my room and lay down to stare at the ceiling and consider all the possibilities. Josie was out working, of course. Junk is never cheap. So I lay and waited for the Blue Nepalese to crawl through the window or paw at the door. I lay awake, wide awake, all evening. I loved that cat and I knew he loved me. Josie came in just before midnight. She lay beside me for a while, tired and dis-spirited. The silence eased a little, I could feel her begin to relax. We looked at each other, tried to smile, glad to have each other there. I might find another cat; and some nights Josie's work wouldn't so dis-spirit her. She put her hand across my forehead, as if reading Braille.

'Come,' she laughed, 'You're my next customer. Let's get fixed.'

Nearby the Grindelallee is the Platenblumen, the flowerpark. And I promised myself I'd make an excuse during the meal, run to the park, and bring Josie back a soft, delicate, bloodred rose. Two. For her dark, Magdalen hair. I never got the chance. Ralph, Peter Ralph, was dead on the floor of his room.

It was then, at that moment, that I had my first junk-horror. Josie searched the room but it was all gone. All of it. I stayed by the door, lost. I looked at Josie's eyes. No. No hope. She couldn't carry junk on her or store it in her room. Customers on their ego-trips complain of this and that and police, ladypolice, as efficient as mother hounds, search everywhere. There would be no junk that night.

I wanted to squat and cry. I was going to hit the ground too hard. I couldn't bear it. I would do anything. I would pray, I would repent, not to hit the ground too hard, for half a dog's chance.

Josie had been down before, hard each time, and sickness and fear already showed on her face.

We went out to a 'phone kiosk. I put in the coin. Josie dialled the number. A pleasant voice in a casual manner explained the maximum and minimum penalties of abuse of this service and advised us of the futility and dangers of making a hoax-call. Then the tape switched off and a girl's voice asked me how it could help me. I couldn't answer. Josie took the 'phone, gave them Ralph's name, the address, the room number, said we were visitors, couldn't stay around now, goodbye. The voice said 'we understand and thank you, please don't be afraid to ...'

Josie put down the 'phone and we started our walks through the streets looking for someone to sell. We knew Ralph's source and we knew he wouldn't sell to us. And I kept thinking of that comfortable voice saying don't be afraid, call us anytime, we can help you. It was a joke. The oldest, dirtiest joke. The only help they could give, junk, they wouldn't give. They had created this supply and demand situation from start to end and from cause to effect. What other planet did that cool, reassured voice come from? We didn't arrange public telephone numbers for domesticated dog-owners so that they could tell us we'd shot their dog, after suitable warnings not to exploit our service with hoax-calls about mid-hits.

We were their game, and going down those streets we knew it.

It's never easy to find junk. Again and again, even when you carry the wherewithal, the watering-holes go dry. You go from one to the other like a confused, wounded animal, frightened every step of the way, sensing the crevices, fearful of exposure, planning your defence to suit each measure of the terrain. If junk only lasted a little longer, or if you could get enough to last a month or a week then you could plan, organise your life. But searching day by day for your very life leaves you waste. You know one day you'll go down, hard and cold. Felled game. And you take on the mentality of only living to avoid death; run run run, until you're running so fast that the best of opportunities fall from your hands and you daren't stop. You run straight into the ground.

That night we found a supplier and we fixed. But the sickness had shaken our souls and the fix only eased the panic. For a few days then I used Josie's business room, disappearing into the corridor whenever a customer visited. The room was used twenty-four hours a day. Each girl, each shift, needed five full-paying customers just to cover her share of the daily rental. Even Otto's heart gave in and he fired me. I was too fretful to work, being forever plagued by the need to know where tonight's fix was coming from. Otto didn't know what was wrong, but like all men of his integrity who had been born straight and had laboured to get some freedom, some time for relaxation into his life, he sympathised with those who were still where he had come from. He offered me a room in his home, and the best food his hausfrau made. That would have me right as rain in next to no time. How could I explain? The straight never believe it is so sick, this sickness for junk, this plead for life. After a few days at Josie's room I had to leave, and I was afraid to go back to the Grindelallee and police questions. Besides I knew I needed the rent money for any junk of any kind from any source. Even losing Josie was robbed of sadness by my need for junk. Having the wherewithal for junk determines your range of partners. I wasn't a very good provider. And to the sellers we had to use I was a hindrance and Josie a moneymaking machine. The sellers were on the street, they could count customers, they could add. And fix Josie's junk at the appropriate price. So she ended up, then, getting no more each day than enough to keep her alive for another day, while still fretful about the next. I lost Josie. I don't know what happened to her. Just like the Blue Nepalese.

The first days and nights on the streets weren't bad. I had some wherewithal and fixed. Then it ended and the signs of scavenging set in.

I was sicker and sicker and more and more dirty and unkempt. I lost all concern for my appearance although I knew it reduced my chances of getting a lead on a fix or fooling a doctor. It just didn't matter. It was not lack of self-respect. I knew my own self and the respect it deserved. It is no mean feat to achieve that knowledge. But the pulsating tremors of my body; the fat, rich waves of horror rolling through my mind; the muscles jerking my limbs or refusing to move, the imminence of the sore hand of death as it leached obscenely at my brain and pawed obscenely for my body; the obscenity of my tormentors, those who regulate the system which reduced me to this, as they passed by washed, fed, well-garbed and shunned me as if I were an accusing ghost haunting with my very presence their callous hypocrisy; the odd eyes that caught mine in a glimpse then flicked away, leaving me of less value to them than a cur. And I just sat, crouched, lifeless, waiting to hit the ground, coiled up inside myself, the horror and sickness pounding my body and mind as I waited to die a hard, cruel unnecessary death. I swore to myself that I was not one of this species, that I was not of this world, would never, never again, want anything of it or to do with it.

A drunkard sat next to me. Another existence. Even he could not understand. He shook his head sadly and in some belated kindness made a gesture of a needle jabbing into an arm. His mouth puckered and his head shook sadly, uncomprehendingly, again. When you see a junky dying give him junk, or give him money, or shoot him through the head. I know what almost all will do. We are a waste disposal problem. You are garbage collectors.

Oh Jesus God give me junk. I will repent, I will pray. I will agree to any barter, but give me junk. I am sitting here begging for what you abhor, what you hate. Why deny it to me? To save yourself? So I traduce your truth to you, your truth to you. What loss is it to you? You can then walk the streets unhaunted, your eyes need not guiltily flick away. I will crawl away out of your sight to walk a whole human being in the daylight. Who gave you the right to guard the doors to my father's mansion? Junkies did not crucify, did not strangle behind the smoke of religions, did not, did not commit the barbarities called history. Your creed did. Your credibility as an accuser is nil. And yet you deny my saviour to me, your laws turn the streets into the road to Calvary, despise me, and demand that I should die and rise again. And even now you still do not know that you cannot even wash your hands after you've solved the waste disposal problem.

The drunkard squeezed my shoulder, then staggered away. I stood up, raised myself with my hands against the wall and leaned on it, pushed myself along, away, in the opposite direction. I found a 'phone box. After the tape switched off the voice asked me if it could help me. It asked again, while eternity passed and trembled in the kiosk. The small panes of glass began breaking as I jerked desperately to hold onto the 'phone.

'I cannot speak.' I said, and the voice asked again if it could help me. I said again, I cannot speak, and the voice whispered 'What?' But I could not speak. I tried, tried to try, then the cable broke from the machine and I fell. More glass broke and the junk sickness began to flow out of my mouth. I thought of Ralph and the scars on his back and his tightening voice explaining how they had hoisted him on crossed spars, pulled the gloved ropes taut so that he could not even wince and how the whip fell, strokes of burning steel upon his back, the sheets of blood flashing across the room at each stroke until there was so much pain he could feel no more pain. How the coat of oily balm was laid over his back by a doctor, and the ropes slackened from his limbs as they lowered him to the ground. And how he swore and promised that he was not a member of the human race. They did not even know he was speaking.

My body began to convult and the door of the kiosk half-opened. The face of Josie came to me, as she stood beside me in the Art Gallery, watching my face as I watched in horror the painting of the Blessed Virgin with the infant Jesus across her knees as she disciplined him with strokes of her adult, human hand. He said he was not of this world. And the day I daydreamed in a school-class, and the red-faced rage of the christian teacher as his strokes fell, the helpless panic which then blackened my mind, as it had before at other hands, and did again and again at other hands, ending with bolts of electricity, as the civilised civilised.

Hands came from behind me and pulled me onto a steel frame and broad, thick straps were fastened around me. I saw the ramp at the back of the ambulance, felt the heave as they pushed from behind, then the jolt as the lever was kicked and the frame folded out into a stretcher. A wet towel rubbed across my face and a voice said: 'What you trying to do? Land without wheels?' Then the daub of wet cotton on my arm and the rescue of the needle and the total flood of life coming back as I fell asleep.

When I awoke I could smell the sweetness of my washed body, the sweetness of the sheets lying over me, the taste of life babynew and delightful in the warmth and safety of the room; and the depthless eternity of relief bright and smiling in my eyes.

On the wall at the end of the bed a plaque hung out with bright orange letters carrying a message from The Machine. It read 'They are poisoning and monopolizing the hallucinogen drugs — LEARN TO MAKE IT WITHOUT ANY CHEMICAL CORN.' Signed, William Burroughs.

I knew I was in the wrong place. They'd never see the point, The Burroughs, the bar-sceners, the classy-hip, the disco-blind, the strut of the high with the extroverted demand in their performances, their demeanour, that others should, ought, to envy them: these people I did not understand. Those who took junk for kicks, not for the paradise of walking whole through the sunlight of the day. I, and Ralph, and Josie, and all the others, took junk to get fixed, literally. That's where the usage comes from, to fix yourself, not to get 'a kick'. We took junk to be whole, to be our potential, be what we were meant to be. That is not a cheap thrill. That is life. Taking junk when you're whole is as vain and stupid as wearing glasses when you've got perfect vision. You'll get a different outlook on what you see, but it's warped and you know it. Maybe that's a dizzying, hip, ain't-it-weird-babe high, like hysterical children in a fun-palace cavorting in front of warped mirrors. Their high, their giggles is for relief at what they know they are not. You can't get high if you're whole, but you might get heady and addicted, like the kids, to your own infatuation in the mirror. I think that often happens. But a blind person's joy on gaining the power of sight is not copyable by closing your eyes for a time, pretending you are blind, and then opening your eyes.

I lay and waited, not wanting to disturb anyone. I had the joy of life in me again. When the key turned in the lock and the door opened I smiled and tried to sit up. But my wrists were bound to the frame of the bed. It didn't matter. The nurse brought a tray of food to the side of the bed and started to feed me, watching me, as I chewed and savoured each mouthful with lionish contentment, nodding my head when he tentatively raised the tea-cup, then chewed again, casually, in Ralph's manner.

When the meal was finished I lay back and slept.

Sometime later they awoke me, released me from the bed, gave me pyjamas and a dressing-gown and took me down the hall to a consulting room. I sat in one of the three armchairs and the two doctors sat opposite me as if, almost, I were interviewing them.

After the preliminaries, as she poured tea for me, the lady doctor began explaining the options. I could go down gradually, the amount of junk reduced slightly every day, as you would reduce a man's normal intake of food. Only one day the reduction is too much, no matter how small, the sickness of starvation hits you, and after that slow death you then still hit the ground hard. Or I could take a substitute, a legal substitute every day for the rest of my life. It would stop the body's craving for junk, stop the brain chemicals wanting junk. It would do no more. This is like stealing your child, giving you another, and telling you the substitute will stop you longing for the first. Or, she said, I could accept the only truth and go down cold straightaway.

I listened. It wasn't worth asking if they would just let me out, give me a daily supply, and let me get on with life.

So I said, yes. Cold.

On the streets the rumour is the eighth day. After that it's all downhill. That's another of the hip lies. It's never downhill. Never. And to this day I don't know what day the slabs of horror stopped, when the mortuary slabs binding my mind eased their grip, when my screams began to blink through their pain and, once, a drop of solace entered. Or when I became aware of the agony of the other two men in the ward. There was a feeling of total brokenness, running brokenness as a new body was congealing from the wreakage and debris of the old, of the odd eternities of thankfulness for a glimpse of peace.

For the first time since the first day I paid some attention to the nurses behind the glass of the partition watching us as nurses watch newborn babes, wondering what universes of dread wrought such havoc in our tortured minds that we arched and strived so insanely against the straps.

Then I awoke in a room again, alone and unbound, and everyone was kind and pleasant to me, as they are to the terminally ill. I was wary of them. But I returned the smiles.

I began to take my meals in the dining-room with other patients; and some doctors and nurses. At my table, in front of my place, a folded rectangle of plastic had my given name written on it. The same applied for the two women and the man with whom I shared the table. The room seemed forever artificially quiet, and we breathed as if the air itself was a threat to us. I noticed that the hand of the girl sitting opposite me would tremble if I looked at her as she raised a cup or a fork to her mouth. Sometimes, when she looked at me, my hand also shook. So we sat and ate in silence, the doctors and nurses occasionally throwing part of their conversations onto our table, or some other patients' table, obliging us to make some gesture of reaction. Mostly we lowered our heads and mumbled. The rein of determination seemed to poison my efforts, all our efforts. But our eyes spoke all the time, unceasingly, between all of us. We knew. Addiction is a far truer word for the emotion of love than the word love. And we knew where our true love lay and that time would never ease this pain of separation that our deaths, our junky-deaths, had caused.

Several times the lady doctor took me into the city. We would stroll through departmental stores, supermarkets, shopping malls, around and about the streets. We took rides on the subway, trips on the buses. Anytime the panic seized me I would squeeze her hand and we would embrace, like longing lovers. If the panic didn't pass we would go back to the car immediately or, if it were too far away, take a taxi.

Gradually I learned to do it alone, but always, always, with cat-like alertness. Then I was released. I'm sorry it was all such a waste; but it was their solution. They taught me to function in the prison of what I was not intended to be. And I had known, I had been, my potential. My eyes often stare out at nothing; while I long to end this exile from my love and live again in my father's manion with my love.

I'm free now. I don't even have to go to the clinic anymore to convince the doubting doctors. I have a room and a job, and I shuffle, stealthily to and fro. And there are many beautiful people to whom I owe all love, all gratitude. Especially to Ralph and Josie. There are also many people to whom I owe all forgiveness. And to my own self I owe an apology, an apology of wasted years. I give it all now.

So now the days pass, unused and meaningless. I skimp and go-without and save. Every so often I steal to the crevices of the city and buy some junk. I store the great wealth in a small room. When I have enough, whenever I have enough if ever I have enough, I will live again; and fix myself for the final run to my saviour's mansion. The wheels will roll, skim, and lift from this hard, cold earth where I am a hapless savage. I will rise into the sweetest blue sky and the doors of my paradise will open. There I will live with that emotion of undying love; my voyage, my journey to a destination, completed.

Fates

WHEN THEY ARE YOUNG their eyes are never so tender. Even in sadness their eyes have the whiteness of anticipation, and eagerly blink from sadness to joy. Always there is the radiance of youth and its soft, ethereal beauty. Tears weep to leave such eyes.

'Your whisky, Sir.' she said, as she placed the glass on the table. Her eyes hovered about, tenderly, over his appearance.

'It is cold tonight, isn't it?' she asked.

'Yes,' he answered, 'I am very cold.' And drank the whisky. 'May I have one more?'

'But you are so young,' she said, 'And you have drunk so much.'

There was laughter, a lilt of happiness, in her voice. She took the glass and walked away, glancing over her shoulder to catch him watching her legs. But he was looking at the years that had hardened the muscles as she walked from customer to customer across the floor of this bar. She was thirty-five, at least.

The street outside was dark. No one passed. Only two other people were in the bar and they each sat hunched in their own company. It was still early evening and the throb of the Paris traffic echoed dimly, but continuously, from the nearby streets.

She stood in front of him; and smiled. It was then that he knew where the tenderness came from: she could see herself through his eyes, and knew he saw so very little; and she was inclined, as one is inclined to instinctively guard a child from falling as it totters on its first steps, to instinctively play the role of woman of the world, who had seen everything and would never toss her head high in girlish contempt for the blunders his unsteady feet might make.

He drank the whisky in one gulp and proffered the empty glass to her. She ignored it and turned away.

'It is easier,' she said, 'to bring the bottle to the glass.'

Walking back to the bar she disinterestedly cuffed one of the other customers on the back: 'Go home, Patrice. Your wife is waiting.'

Patrice looked over at him and winked, then rose and left. She had a lot to teach, that was obvious, but she knew less than she assumed.

'My name is Angela,' she said, and then efficiently explained the gradients on the tape measure stuck to the bottle. She looked at his appearance once more.

'You'll be able to pay for this?' she asked.

'For what I drink, yes.'

She looked hurt, suddenly, and very vulnerable.

'My name is Emmet,' he said and tried to smile his repentance.

'You have a beautiful name,' she said. She said it dispassionately, but with her eyes so sheltered that he knew she saw a child who might, without warning, say something frightening.

'I'm sorry, Angela. I am a little drunk.'

'Oh blay blay,' she said. 'It is not important. Watch.'

He watched as she took the ring of keys from under her apron and opened the top of the juke-box. She smiled happily at him and began pressing buttons. There was a famine in her eyes, a famine of the years gone, their only harvest a few memories. And some had not even that. But he knew she could see the same through his eyes. She felt it, more than ever, through his eyes. That was why she had this attentiveness to him, as if she had something she had to prove to him.

'Come, Emmet. I want to dance with you.'

To stand would be difficult, walking impossible, but to dance would be good — if only he could get from the table without heaving over. He remembered to hold his spine straight and to walk as if he intended to go ten paces further than where he was going. She caught him, laughed, and put her arms around him. She was warm and soft, and, when he looked down at her eyes he thought, for a moment, that he saw a young, giggling girl in his arms. He smiled.

'Imagine, Angela, I shall be able to tell my grandchildren that I danced with the most beautiful woman in Paris when I was twenty.'

She looked away.

'You are too young to speak of having grandchildren.'

And he realised how stupid and tactless he was. Immediately she looked up at him and saw his regret.

'Oh blay blay. It is not important,' she said and squeezed, 'It is winter outside and warm in here and I like you.'

'Why?'

'I was born in Paris, Emmet. Paris has always been my home. Even if I know no one I at least know the stones on the streets. You would not be so lonely if you could say that.'

'No. I suppose not.'

It was the only thing to say. She had come very close to injuring him. He knew he was a stranger in their home, a step-child to their mother tongue awash and scenting the air; enviously gazing, wide-eyed, through the blurred glass of their clean, graceful language. And the incommunicable, unebbing feeling of loneliness.

'Why have you come to Paris?'

'Just to leave another place.'

'You were unhappy in England?'

He began to laugh and she, puzzled, stopped dancing and, at arms-length, gazed at him.

'Tell me,' she smiled, 'Why are you laughing?'

'Because I know you think Irlande is another bewildering, English eccentricity.'

For a moment the tenderness came back into her eyes. She smiled sympathetic.

'I understand, Emmet. Please wait. I'll make some coffee.'

He sat back at the table no longer laughing but feeling he had said something that was clever, but also boyish and cute. For spite he raised and drank from the bottle, then examined the tape to see how much the gulp had cost him. He was running out of more money than he could afford at every sip.

She put the cup in front of him and said: 'Straight down.' He obeyed. It hit his stomach, and then his entire body, with the heavy lethargy of an unfriendly punch.

'Angela!' He folded his arms on the table, drooped over, and slept.

*

She shook him awake. A lot of the drunkenness had passed. He went to the toilet, for comfort to the ladies' toilet, and suffered philosophically the awful mess his body made. He washed and regretted the scruffiness of his jacket, his unwashed shirt. Otherwise he looked well. Anyway, he would pass.

The bar was closed now. The only light came through the door from the corridor running alongside the back of the counter. Angela was going around the bar adding unnecessary touches to the tidiness. The bottle had been taken away, but he could see the amber glint in the glass on the table.

'What was that stuff you gave me, Angela?'

'It's good, hmm?'

'It had eggs in it?'

'Yes. And olive oil. Didn't you taste that?'

'Of course, Angela. Of course.'

The whisky was finished, the bar needed no more touches of nervous tidiness. Any words he might say seemed to turn him into a beggar; and silence made him a supplicant.

'Why did you come to Paris in winter?' she asked with the accuracy of irrelevance. He started.

'I'm just looking for somewhere. And I stopped here.'

'Come. I must close up.' She directed him into the hall, then turned to lock the door.

'I live on the top floor, the fourth floor.' She took his arm and they began climbing the stairs.

'It's a very small apartment,' she continued. 'The owner lets me have it cheap because I work in the bar.'

'Oh. I thought you were the owner.'

'No, no. I am a worker.'

And they silently climbed the rest of the stairs.

The apartment door led straight from the landing into a narrow kitchen. A door just before the window led to the only other room. It felt warm after the long climb. He took off his jacket. The strangest thing about the room was that it had no chairs. A bed, yes, and a wardrobe, but to sit, nothing only an assortment of cushions around the tiny floor area. He let his jacket fall gently onto the floor. She smiled, amused at his failure to understand how much more free the room was without chairs. And so much more homely. She sat, and patted the floor beside her: 'Sit here.'

He did. She put her arms about his neck and kissed him, nonchalantly, perfunctorily, her lips plucking about his mouth and face, yet gently, with a longing, a softness. He put his hands under the sides of her sweater and her body rose, like a swan's, and the sweater slipped over her head. Her hand dipped, a magic wand, and unbuttoned his shirtfront. Again she kissed his mouth, then unclasped her bra and pressed herself to him.

'You are so warm,' she said, 'So warm.'

There is a legend, a pagan legend from the beginnings of mankind, of ancient, hungry savages clustered together in the jungle mist to grunt and mourn for the fallowness of their youth. And their groaning moved and heaved and swayed; and broke into a scream, a long, life-worn scream of pain that screamed their despiration; a scream pitched higher than their need could hear, a force of life that bound them silent. And in the quietness, in longing, none could hear his own scream. And the force of life clawed and kicked and screamed for salvation. A woman appeared, a hideous chastisement of bare, raw, unknown flesh sickened with the blight of strangeness. And each recoiled, revolted, at the power of their longing. And she sobbed to them: Me! Me!

'I want you,' she said, and the power and challenge of her body crushed against him.

In the legend they stared in awe, and trembled. The creature curled and the mass of sickness sickly cried: ME! They stood, bound, and distantly heard a groan crying in the mist. Then a trembling hand of pity reached out; and touched her.

Angela opened her legs and as Emmet entered her she raised her knees and her body lifted to him. Her head hanging back, her eyes closed, her open mouth gasping for air and longing, she pulsated in a sheen of sweat against him.

Legend says the terrified hand reached out, and touched. And raised the hand to his mouth and kissed it. And fearfully raised his bowed head to look into her eyes. His eyes looked and set, struck, at the beauty of the girl before him. The beauty of her face, the beauty of her hair, the beauty of her body, the beauty of her eyes. No eyes had ever seen such beauty, no ears had ever heard such beauty, no words had ever spoken such beauty. A meadow Spring of beauty.

Angela lay quiet, and with distant, saintly tenderness, patiently held Emmet's still heaving body.

In the legend they smiled secretly at each other. No one knew they smiled. And his eyes said to his friends: look how beautiful she is. But a laugh twisted madly in their screams, and they played with their hands, and changed in their stance, discomforted. They could not see. And they left them.

'Where is your home, Emmet?' she asked.

'I have none.'

'No? It must be sad, then.'

'It doesn't matter to me.'

'Paris seems to hold so many like that. Even its own, like me.' She pushed his head away and looked into his eyes: 'There is someone who loves you, somewhere?'

'I don't know. It's not important.'

'No?'

'Is that why we live?'

'Oh blay blay,' she answered, 'That is silly.'

'Angela, you know the state of my clothes. You saw all of the money I have in the world when I paid for the drink. There is no door anywhere in this world that I can pass through except by invitation or forebearance. What more do you want me to say?'

'How long will you stay in Paris?'

'Day by day. I don't know.'

'And when the money is gone?'

'Dosshouse walls.'

She sighed. 'You have been in that situation before?'

'I was born in a similar house.'

She moved herself underneath and kissed his forehead.

'I will bring you a drink,' she said, and slipped out from under him. He sat up, turned, and moved to rest his back against the attic window. Paris looked silent, except for the beam of headlights lacing through the streets.

She came back and squatted opposite him against the window. He took the tumbler, clinked it against hers, and drank.

'I often sit here alone at night. It gives me peace. Look. Look at the streets. They have heard the rage of so many revolutionaries and the tramp of so many armies. I can even make-believe, some nights, that I hear the neighing of the horses in the garrisons. The shout of challenge to a passing stranger. And the tread of the great who walked on the stones of these streets.'

Emmet gazed at her, enraptured at the beauty of her language. He reached for her sweater and passed it to her.

'Put it on, Angela. I don't want you to catch cold.'

She smiled that tender, vulnerable smile: 'Emmet you are so, so . . . so much typical of an English eccentricity.'

'I don't mind. I care for you, Angela.'

'How typical. Typical. You are head over heels in love with me and you say: "I care for you, Angela." '

'No, Angela. I am not in love with you.'

She turned and looked out the window: 'It is peaceful to think and reflect, Emmet. To watch the clouds in the sky, to listen to the silence. It is nourishment to me, to see the night sealing this day, and all the days past. And to have a young man beside me with the ethereal fragrance of youth in his charm. And to hear the lost sadness in your voice. That is why I wanted you. Men who speak with the feel of sadness know. They do not take a woman by greed and smugness, but with the passion of need, and the compassion of the humility of need. They have known many nights of yearning in a sleeping city. I have seen so many men in the bar and so few know. They think the only importance is to make a woman laugh. They are grown, grown men. And they do not know the difference between a girl and a woman.'

They sat in silence, each hoping that a chance word would bring comfort, and seal the past between them.

'In pagan mythology there is a legend, Angela, that love is self-adulation. We love others for what we see of ourselves in them.'

'Perhaps they are right.'

'In that way, yes, I love you.'

'Blay blay, Emmet. That is not love. That is patriotism. That is how I love Paris.'

She tipped the bottle and filled his glass, then her own. Straight whisky. They looked at each other, with half smiling faces, and regretful, concerned eyes.

'So, Emmet . . .' and she raised the glass to her lips and drank until the glass was empty. He copied suit, and she refilled the glasses.

'I have a feeling, Angela, of finned missiles hovering overhead, hovering over our heads like crucifixes, anointing the about-to-die.'

'You are going to leave me, Emmet?'

'We are going to leave each other, Angela.'

She smiled, almost coquettishly: 'Now I know what they mean about the serpent eating its tail.'

Their relief flooded out in laughter, and he watched her, through his laughter, drain the last of the whisky from her glass. The bravery and splendour of her dignity belittled him and he, too, drained his glass. She watched him, watched him try to summon dignity and as she leaned over to gently touch his face he spoke, and the words startled her.

'I wish I were you, Angela.'

'Emmet you are being silly again,' she caught his arm: 'You gave me what I wanted. I am not a young girl trying to embed a hook of guilt in you. I know there is no guilt in love unless it is the rape of love you call patriotism. I wanted you. I wanted to prove to you you needn't look far to find someone to love you.'

She went on in an endless stream of language, ringing out word after word after word. It was beautiful to watch her animation, and he began to understand her.

She was not a woman you would find cloistered behind convent walls, where women might come face to face with their existence if they did not pray; nor a woman cloistered behind the veil of marriage, where women become as openly epigrammatic as nuns. Angela had no veils, no facade. This was the source of her dignity and its strength. This was the source of her tenderness and empathy for others. She knew how easy it would be to enter a mirage, and make-believe it was true.

'And always, Emmet, life carried me along. I thought I would be no different to anyone. But slowly the world seemed to gather itself to itself, and I became a bystander. All the pressures which had washed around me slowly disappeared. I was alone. It seemed I had lived no day in the past; each day had died on me, and I faced a life of mourning. I was thirty then. And if I said I did not see it happen, or would not change it if I could, my companions looked strange at me and thought I lied. And they changed towards me, and slowly left me.'

She smiled, a bright sparkling smile of anticipation.

'Have you noticed in France so many women wear dour black clothes. They say it is becoming. Are they the same in Ireland?'

'In intent, yes. But I don't really remember about the colours.'

He held out his glass for a refill.

'It will be so late, Emmet. You'll have to sleep here.'

' I understand.'

She re-filled his glass: 'You see, tonight, you've brought the past alive for me. I like that. That's why I like you.'

He didn't smile. He lowered his eyes and examined the whisky.

'There's a ticket in my pocket, Angela. From the State pawnshop. What does that say about the future?'

'I don't know. What did you pawn?'

'My suitcase.'

'And they took it?'

'He rummaged through it like a customs inspector and took the lot.'

'Emmet, Emmet,' she tipped up his chin. 'That says a great deal for the future.'

She seemed amused and pleased at the thought of him casually pawning his suitcase at the State pawnshop. Yet it wasn't a casual affair. They ask for identity cards and proof of ownership of the item being pawned. Convincing a French civil servant that your suitcase is your own is no casual matter. Angela was now shaking with mirth. She took his glass and drank a little. And almost convulted trying to keep the whisky in against her laughter.

'Come to bed, Emmet. Come to bed.'

They went to bed and made love. Occasionally their eyes would meet and immediately she would brim over again with laughter. Eventually his face had to loosen, and he smiled back. It was of no importance. The clean bed was warm and cosy and Angela beautiful, tender, and caring. In such situations life's humiliations are the antics of a clown, to be laughed over and enjoyed. When he closed his eyes to sleep her serenity and dignity and bravery, and her smiling love, gave him a comfort and a joy he had never known before.

*

Three hours later, at five o'clock, she shook him awake. Bleary, with the cold reality of the morning creeping over him, he washed himself as best he could in the kitchen. But no amount of scrubbing could wash away the scruffiness of his unshaved face. She gave him one of her sweaters and it changed his appearance to one of debonair and healthy naturalness. She counted out some money on the table. So much for a one-day bus ticket, so much for coffee. Then she explained to him the points around the city where the black — the unregistered, uninsured — labour is hired.

'You will have to fight with them, Emmet. One hundred francs, eight hours, never less, walk away. And let them see you will go berserk if they do not pay you at the end of the day, or pay you less. They are hard, rough, heartless people. You must pretend you have a lot of friends — male friends, in Paris. That it will not be worth the trouble to cheat you. Some people say some of the police are in their pay. You understand? Try to make friends so that you will be in a group at the end of the day. And watch for the spies during the day asking you questions to see how vulnerable you are to need or intimidation. Watch the hiring-agent and watch those who have any rapport with him. It's only a few days and we'll find something better. When you come back come straight here, not into the bar.

They drank some coffee, then she kissed him and went back to bed. And Emmet, thoroughly frightened, nervously walked down the stairs and out onto the threatening streets.

A milk delivery van was coming, in stops and starts, up the street. Emmet saw Patrice jumping out to nimbly place bottles on window sills and against doors. Patrice saw Emmet, and paused. They came alongside and Patrice's lecherous face grinned. He bent his arm, half-raised it to his shoulder and shook its clenched fist: 'Arrgh,' he grunted, 'I've been trying to get that bitch for months.' And his face grimmaced.

Emmet stared till Patrice's face straightened.

'You were well-named Patrice,' he said, and threw one of Angela's coins at his feet: 'Go buy a drink.'

'English asshole,' Patrice answered, and lightly climbed into the van and drove away.

Emmet walked on, then stopped and turned back. He picked up the coin and slipped it into his shoe as a keepsake. Someday, perhaps, he would tell a radiant child that she was the most beautiful little girl in Paris. And she was there and she was so because he had danced with the most beautiful woman in Paris when he was twenty. He would give her the coin and they would smilingly look at each other.

The dreams of youth are strange.

The Search

IT'S A SHABBY ROOM. An old room in an old house: a mass of creaking boards and threadbare, dust-packed carpets. Yellowing walls of cracked, peeling paint and relics of black, gleaming, dirt-greased furniture. And in this room, a couch against one wall; a shelf hanging from the opposite one. Nothing there but a book, prostrate and open. And on the couch the huddled figure of the unkempt character, his wrinkled face bristled and dirty. But now, as he is elicited for you, he sits up and rubs his old, worn face, shuddering like a cat, in pleasure.

'Aaaah! It's cold these nights . . .'
And so it is: at three o'clock in the morning, as he reaches down and rubs his naked toes.

'Merciful God. It'd take the breath away from a man.'
Another shudder, and the skin sucks into the gaunt, hairless skull.

'I'll light the fire in a little while and roast for an hour. Hey! won't I!'
And his gummy jaws squash and grin at the big toe being caressed.

'Hey! Alexander! Won't that please you!'
And his big toe smiles blandly back, its face ashine.

'Haa? And how's my little one, Lolita, heh? Trust that Goldsmith to be standing beside you and you cuddling in underneath him. Mind you, me dear, if you ever find an extra hand cuddling the both of you you'll know that'll be Danton. He's the middle toe, hehe! And then, God love us, standing beside the Great, is the sad Longfeller. That's me little, left foot.'

The old man could not speak so clearly to you, but in his mind he knows them all well, and he chortles to himself.

'Heeheehee. Nice little toes, snarled little toes, good little toes, heeheehee.'

And he giggles, chortling to himself, rocking himself back and forth. Then slowly he sobers, drawing in his breath.

> 'Sure who minds an old man talking to himself in the middle of the night. Who minds at all. And there no one else worth talking to anyway.'

His laughter squeaked out and ended, like a little patter of summer rain.

> 'George! George!'

George, she called, George, across the peaceful fields and the quilted browns and greens of the sun's evening hue.

> 'You'll always be needing looking after, you will, that's a fact.'

And her head shook and the breeze cuffed her hair across her face.

> 'Always. Even when you're a man.'

Resigned, now, she was. Resigned to it all, since the distance, mellow sadness had fallen like a mantle across her life. She took the fishing tackle and laid it on the window sill.

> 'Boy don't you know you'll never catch anything if you file the barb off the hooks.'

Ah, but who wanted the fish anyway. Only to sit by the river in those long-dead days: with the friendliness of solitude under the open skies.

Then dinner was over; over and forgotten, nestling comfortably in the stomach with warmth and energy and contentment.

> 'Don't ever let them know you don't like to kill.'

And she smiled. And the needles ducked in and out of the line of wool.

> 'You have to respect their values, George. One day you're going to have to survive them – on your own.'

Yes. And survive you, the old man remembered. We learn that lesson first at mother's hands.

Then the evening was still, and the white summer light of the moon was upon the stage of the cottage, waiting: haunting the fields to silence, and the cottage and the wind as the dawning adolescence's chaos struggled against the night closing in about him, smothering him in its arms, as gently, as inexorably, as the mothering, breathless, confining love and confining night settling to squeeze the savagely heaving mind to a soundless pitch of madness.

> 'You know I mean the best for you.'

The bobbin of wool tumbled about on her lap as the wayward move of her hand unravelled more line.

> 'Sure you're great company for me, lad, in your auld, meandering way; with that fine, mysterious world you've spun about you. And you being abiding and sorely patient and conforming to keep

the dreamless adults a far, far arm's length away.'

They smiled, then, while the night closed in with harmony and peace together about them. And his leaping, fish-like soul dived calmly to the depths to nurse itself in sleep. The old man laughed.

'Heeheehee, but different arms and different lengths.'

Thus the moonfaced teacher stood aghast.

'And what did you say you did on the weekend?'

'Strangled the cat with me hands, Sir, I did. Broke its neck, Sir.'

'Did you now?'

Said he, looking impressed above his black soutane and shining, white collar.

'And what made you do that?'

'Ah, sure she ate the fish I caught, didn't she, Sir.'

'Ah. Ah. I see.'

So the fatal surviving began as it must, as counselled, with lies, and respect for doomed values: interchanged.

The old house, in another country, creaked with the wind. And the promise of at least purgatory.

'It's nearly a lie to teach children the whole truth in a wholly truthful way.'

The moonface said, at the depth of his profundity, and faded away to the grave he surely is in now.

*

The old man rubbed his chin.

'Sure, what's the harm, talking. Takes my mind off the cold and it so dark and lonely in here with the auld, melancholy moon hushing the dark and troubled skies outside. It's the kind of night I could take to the drink. Aye, gladly take to the drink. Talk to myself, aye, get some communication with meself.'

He sighs. And the sigh is sad and unsettling, pity. Pity.

'Shut up.'

Pity. Weeping Pity.

'Shut up, I said, shut up.'

Drooling, sloppy pity.

'They think it's passive, they do. Not manly. They'd have you extrovert a big, bellowing lust for life. Aye, lust for life. Strike hard and cut a passage out for yourself with your figure. Great vision of health, that, for them. Fine figure of a man. Bah!'

He sighed again, and lapsed into memory. Brush strokes of memories leading inexorably to more memories, back and forth, broken and unbroken across the canvas of his life as it hung, a clouded painting of his mind; the silent, solemn, gravel paths of the museum subdued in respect as the footfalls fall gently and pass on; walking, inexorably, to their grave.

'A match, a match, and I'll light this bloody fire.'
The ornate cylinders of porcelain flamed with gas as the match struck, and the flames died down.

'Merciful God.'
And his hands patted around the meter and jabbed a coin into the slot.

'A man would need a bloody shovel to feed you.'
He kicked the meter as if it were a human thing. With anger.

'What human hand would take that money from me.'
And he pounded the meter again.

'There's one as will, there is, there's one as will.'
He paused; then rested, crouching into himself, the futility of his sadness known to him.

'A . . . a . . . a drug. A drug to rob this mind of memories. Oh to wash the canvas clean with alcohol. Death, didn't Danton call you his friend if you promised to do this.'

The sadness was deep, flowing quickly over crevices worn smooth with previous sorrow, flowing quick to the heart of his spirit. And her voice echoed again.

'You're the last from the nest; the last to leave me.'
And the boy lowered his eyes, so that she should never know, the many times I hated and longed to be gone, when you poised to hurt, oh, for goodness' sake, for want of discipline, in correction's name, the firm, deliberating, unconscious pause between the poise and the striking: and the glimpse of its obscenity before the reddening distrust flowed between us; the slap of rape, the odourless smell of incest. And under the eyes, the leaving has a great lining of joy to it. Glad, glad, glad to be going from the warm, loving nest. Who needs whom? Glad, glad; glad to be gone, away, to yet another school.

The quagmire receded as the spirit that named his toes rallied to save him. Back on the couch he lies, comfortably, in the growing warmth of the room: and his legs float joyfully up, the wriggling toes dancing in the fire's glow.

'How do I answer? Which child I love most. Look at this accused hand: Which finger would I rather lose?'

He watched his toes wriggle as shadows on the wall and rubbed his bristling beard in merriment.

'I'm glad I have you, toes, I am. If one of you went missing I'd stumble heavily, with grief: stumble heavily, and God Almighty knows who or what I'd plod over in my talented anguish: or how high and glorious I'd rise with the immaculate roars of my screams.'

The emotion and the logic met, in collision: the birth of drama, sheared of poetry. And he slumps back into the feeling of the troubled skies ready to heave and open; the utter coldness of the world so barren to his groping love of it.

'Ah, but ah . . .'

And he exhales so totally . . .

The dead smell of memories, clouding over the canvas, and I no longer knowing where it was I came alive into life, emerged new-grown into life; splashed joyful as a child and threaded time as if it were water, watching for a course. Nor when it was it seemed I had fallen asleep in life and then awoke, startled, drifting into the nothingness of death.

The old man knew the feelings in his mind, but the words and feelings never mirrored each the other: never struck and abrazed to flame a glow of comprehension on the stagnant, heavy swamp of vast, vague feelings defying the thin paint of words.

'But, ah, I . . . I . . . I . . .'

He looks around, feeling a stale disgust with himself settle like greased dirt on his mind. Before his eyes see and latch to the magic of the book and he begins to move as rapidly as he sees it. He rises, steps, trips: the cry of anguish as pure and intense as the pain as he slumps to the floor where he sprawls and the air rushes in gasps in-and-out of his lungs.

'Ah God. Ah sweet, holy God!'

And the broken toe throbs. He feels it: raises his arm to backhand a tear: and swears. And begins to rally.

'I'll have to put you in a brace, little toe, hm? Bind you up. Now isn't that hard for all the good intended? Or I could cut you off, kaput. But there are other needs . . .'

And he giggles silently with the words.

'Other needs. Who needs whom? Blessed be thou, little toe, that I may bear thee, and thou, little toe, shall bear me.'

And he giggles deep down in himself.

'Heehee. Aren't we a great, bloody comedy, altogether.'

And in the age-old fashion the childish tears and pain are forgotten and he warms to his own infatuation.

'A tot. I think I'll take sup a tot.'
And he giggles again with the merriment of age.

'I'm poor, God knows, but I can afford a sup.'
So he crawls back to his couch to find the bottle and sip its burning anodyne into his worn body while he listens as her voice emerges.

'Would you take a drink, Mr. Shaw?'
The mourner nodded.

'Fine man he was. A very fine man indeed. May God comfort you in your loss.'
The spirits drained from the glasses as the mourners stood in whispering groups.

'But sure. You've a fine lad there to look after you.'
The mourner comforted while the fine lad waited, bored to piousness.

'Easy, boys, now. Easy.'
The mourner instructed as they handled the father's body into the coffin.

'There we are now. That's it.'
He smoothed out the shroud. The priest stepped forward to chant the prayers; and the purging began, to be re-lived endlessly, well remembered by an old man.

'Bloody fine dramatists, those fellows, with their lamentations.'
Broken mumblings answered the invocations; rising, falling, coughing; the slow, creeping, subdued uniformity of prayer swaying back and forth over the body, hypnotising the room for the birth of holy silence.

Then it was over. Ended. One by one the mourners approached the coffin, touched the clenched, marble-cold fists, murmured, and stepped back, their hands gesturing the Sign of the Cross over themselves.

She bowed, kindly, concerned; brushed the fine lad's head and whispered.

'Go up and say goodbye to your father, now. Say it yourself, mind you.'
A great tingle of sweet sadness mingled through the mourners: Ah God bless you now, look at him. And a tear would have trembled them into wailing. Their eyes and stance turned the death-room into a stage as they held their breath for the play on drama to enter, stealthily, its well-loved ending.

'Go on, now. Go on. They're waiting for you.'
The actor failed to appear. The room murmured with the unexpected

excitement of the pause. —— Ah look! He can't move, ah God love him. Look at him —

'Go on, for shame. Look at the priest lookin' at you.'

The tension mounted. This might be something now, begod, you never could tell. He might renege.

Then the minutes passed; the silence deepening as the mother prodded the son forward in the silence that turned brazen and bright in its coldness, chilling the room to consciousness, the expectancy trembling at the consciousness of the great unknown that stood, and lay, and faced them. Till her quick, determined, no-nonsense strides struck upon the boards and her lips well-kissed the corpse. Strange glances struck the boy as the coffin was closed.

Wouldn't kiss his father! God! We know what that is. And the coffin closing for the last time too.

> 'He did nothing to merit that gesture of love. And there is no more to be said but that.'

She whispered with a strange sorrow.

> 'What's to become of you now. That will mark you in this parish and the parishes beyond and no parent will be . . .'

> 'There's no end to comprehension. There's an end to understanding, to empathy. The former decreased the latter. That was healthy. Normal. And a chasm dug gladly, gladly, around me, for a solace I needed and sought and found. And all without that solace were strangers: too far away to ever be touched. There is no more to be said but that.'

He was mellow now; open, understanding. Older. Seeing more than a child. Seeing the opal skies and the summer flowers gloriously grown free and graceful and swaying playfully in the face of the dour, ocean breeze, their bright colours a bouquet around the happiness of the ancient village, so many, many years before, when she came into womanhood, liltingly.

> 'O 'twas fine to be a young girl and to have the twinkle of a boy's eye. And he being well respected all about. A fine upstanding, healthy, young man and the laughter free and blossoming in the still, evening's air. Oh and the pride of the banns of marriage being read, it be like you be a great traveller to foreign places and they be plodding about the same auld acres like the cattle. A great adventure starting and they being envious of you. Drugged with mad, blind happiness and contentment that might last a lifetime, or seep as slowly and gently away as the tide and

leave a body set well and firm in life; well able to ride out the storms to the end.'

The old man nodded, and sipped on the bottle. Clear as spring water I see it still. And the buffeting, here and there, through life; the years greedily crawling over me, an old man, storm-beaten and dying in this shabby, dirt-creviced room. An old man dying: just the actor impersonating me, dying; after imprisoning me for all of my life, a persona at the other side of the chasm, to face the world: someone else fooling the world that he was really me. And yet another persona, his own, to play the red herring and fool me too. Ah, but not when I drowned the chasm with drink and floundered out to pinion that hypocrisy that ate and talked as if it were really me. Then I did the bloody talking and ateing I did. And the sound sleeping afterwards too. Ah yes I did.

The old man lying on the couch shivered and moaned.

'But I'd wake up stranded back inside the chasm, trembling: glad, glad, to take asylum and lie proned in the chasm's refuge. And this, this hypocrisy would slowly start talking and ateing and living for me again.'

Whisky often made the old man talk like that. It made him feel good; funny; the way we are fulfilled. Besides one day I won't be here. I'll be dead. Gone. But it won't be me. I'll be extinct. A body rotting in the ground with nothing of me in it. Meantime I gape: funny; to gape, held pinned as still as a corpse to this fool's crippled, broken mumblings. And to feel the pain and humiliations as he stumbled and pushed through the years to leave me here. There's the epitaph: it wasn't really me at all.

Ask her.

'Do you think now, Mr. Shaw, it would be best for him to be off in another school?'

The mourner flexed the spirit around the glass and drank.

'Well . . .'

And he smiled at the boy backing out of earshot.

'Well . . .'

He said. And it faded away to a response his lips never formed, while she smiled.

'Sometimes I think he's a ghost himself the way he creeps about.'

And she smiled as the boy disappeared mutely into the mourners back from depositing the coffin in the graveyard.

Had a great sense of occasion in those days: the mourning and the drinking and the re-making of friends over the dead.

'Ha! Is that what you're staring at!' bellowed the stout Mulvahy of the Empty-House Restaurant as the boy backed into him.

'Is it Cafferty's strip of a daughter you're gawking at? Ah boys now.' said he to the men-boys, as they lowered their pints of porter in unison. 'I bet now he'd do that one as aisy as feeding carrots to a donkey.' And the hearty laughter chorused from the group as he placed an arm around the boy's shoulders. And whispered, softly: 'So you wouldn't kiss the ghost.' Then loudly his oath cut a swath of silence through the noise of the wake: 'And you'll be shagging ghosts all your life, God save us.' And he laughed into his disappearing porter against the hushed embarrassment of the men-boys. And a great, great mocking rang in his laugh.

'A guzzler for the drink that man was. Always kept his chasm full. Walking on porter, steady as a rock.' The old man nestled the whiskey on his tongue, eyes closed. Sweet dew on grass. Morning's dawn daubed with the dead of night, furrows of clouds tinged by the coming day; and the waiting for the great doors to open and admit the young man to the halls of learning. The solitude of books and the triumph of study; heady happiness to an eager mind. Glorious months of solitude before a young girl's flippancy drew back another curtain.

>'Aren't you the quiet one! And as content as the cat coming and going without a word. Sure no one knows you at all!'

The melody opened as sweetly as the shy smiles that peeped out of the eyes and spread wide across their faces.

>'Are you shy of me then?' And she taunted, blossoming.

>'Terribly immature, you know, boys are, to be nervous of us. God if they only knew!'

It never touched their lives. Knowledge. They read, they listened, they retained, and locked away the wealth in a vast, empty corner of their minds. They stored knowledge, aye, but never understood it. It never bothered them. They learned as if learning a trade, the knowledge useful only as a profession, irrelevant and touchless to their feelings and desires: never absorbed into part of their being.

>'It's lovely here isn't it?'

Envy was aroused by her beautiful calmness, the clarity and peace of mental health in smiling depthless eyes.

>'I'm grand and happy here you know.'

Oh, for a sign that learning wondered at the back of those eyes.

>'Do you not want to talk to me then?'

>'I believe school romances childishly immature.'

'But this isn't school at all, lad, don't you know. It's university.'
'Please, young lady, let's not dauble in semantics.'
'Wow! Hear you!'
'Besides, I doubt of your willingness to entice being capable of transformation into the willingness to give of that which you flatteringly believe entices.'
'Good God! You're odder than I thought.'
'Please. Don't be pedantic.'

That brought a great laugh altogether it did. But sure I didn't know about the wars of this and that, despite all I knew I knew. And all the hustling and jockeying and preening and pushing about into an ancient order as they paired off to raise their young about the cities and the world leaving me musing, lost. There was something I hadn't learned: or an instinct rendered fatuous by learning.

The great doors swung closed behind a young man shrouded in a mist of dim, unformed learning: and the forming fear that the world would never let him hold what he had so joyfully absorbed.

The old man stirred on the couch.

'It's an eerie night, God knows. If the gas holds I'll see the day gladly. Hate the light to go with the fire gone and the great flush of callous want flooding the room colder than it is. Like a strange, solid hand falling hard on your back.'

'Ah God man could you spare a drink!'

The trembling voice broke as the trembling hand fell on the back and the body staggered after it, hitting square on the shoulder.

'Ah God I'm sorry sir. I need a drink badly. Sir.'

And the vacant eyes of Mulvahy stared out at him.

The glass was raised and a concentration brushed back the empty deadness from the face as the crippled apology for being receded; just for that moment, till the empty glass flushed it back again. The casing was gone. The drink flowed in but the man never straightened, standing hulked against the bar, the eyes wandering weakly about, searching for their master. In this refined bar, where young ladies come to sip alcohol I never thought their healthy minds needed.

'Well look who it is! George! How are you! It must be years...'

Good God, said Mulvahy, staggering away. A man like you, Sir. Cohorting with redundant housewives. And she smiled at the silly drunk.

'You must come out and visit us sometime. We've three children now, you know. You'd never believe it, would you.

I heard Mulvahy groan, and turned, and caught her sensible eyes darting unknowingly twixt myself and Mulvahy.

'The youngest has a great resemblance to you, you know, emotionally.'

The beautiful smile again, the soft, womanly tenderness, the bottled-up, high-pitched nuance of her accent; and the thrilling, feminine perfume about the shining, hard glass of her dazzling radiance, the clustered skin preserved deep inside: too deep to be ever touched or loved.

You couldn't help smiling back, with a wondering sadness, for her. Then the bare shambles of Mulvahy silhouetted against the frosted window of the bar, then passed away. He never knew to whom he spoke.

'I hear you're getting odder and odder, praise be, and you not looking a day older at all. Do you never be thinking now it's time you settled down.'

She rambled away with the words to sketch in the years drawn bright and easy as the langurous, flowing sea: as beautiful as the sounds of the sea hushing against the shore, and the mystery in its beauty as strange and startling as her realisation that she talked into a chasm of rudeness, of a loneliness that couldn't speak.

The parting was blameless, and blessed with smiles to hide the shame and regret. Two children staring at the two strange adults they had become. And both knew, one had not learned, or one lacked, something. Nothing but a trite word for a mystery. Something. As they looked into each other's eyes, in panic, wondering who: wondering what life had been lost. And in my fear I stumbled out under her eyes; out into the night, down the roads, into the pubs, the ghost of Mulvahy's reflection of himself in the frosted surge of the glass from bar to bar: the quietly, hysterical eyes sounding for depth in each stranger's eyes. Sitting drunk and inwardly warm on the stone steps in the blackness of the night; night after night. Not dirty enough to accept, but accepting, the smell of his own stench; washing their untrue reality away with any drink while Danton's words kept ringing in my ears: 'there was a mistake in our creation, something was left out. But we won't find it by pawing in each other's innards'. He shouted it to Phillippeau: 'Life isn't worth the trouble it takes to keep it going'. Oh if I too could study a respectable end from the drunkenness of the stone steps, to lead me out of my own Gethsemane, but not on the road to Calvary. It shouldn't have to end that way. So you stay in the Garden of Gethsemane, hysterically pawing your own innards for its reason. To others, a penance, and you glad of the drink that absolves them of it.

The gas and the light were holding out for the old man, actor and reactor, in the old room in the old house.

> 'The auld toe is hurtin' me. Ah but it's a contented auld night just the same. A little, little sip on the bottle now, and a drag on a cigarette in the warmth and a bit of musing to meself here and there and sure I don't mind at all a bit of pain. Rub it a little bit and sort of be coaxing meself out of it.'

Long gone the days of fishing tackle in the evening's great hue of colours, the spinning of line along the currents and the ancient, repeated warnings from the fishermen:

> 'Don't look down at yourself in the water, lad. It'll make you enfeebled, light-headed, lad. Y'might drown before you know it...'

Ah, the little tricks you can find, to draw a curtain of an answer over a question. Gethsemane is a pool in the garden of the mind. And you mustn't go fishing there, lad.

> 'And Calculus, sure, is just another Roman general.'

Replied Mulvahy at the wake when the Canon glared.

The little, unconscious dramas of comedy, bring resignation, and mellowness, to the Gethsemane of present memories, if the burning dread in the stomach quickens you enough to catch them. And you catch an eye, as eyes first met, aeons ago, blinked, and saw themselves, and the common bond of the burning dread that haunts each. And turned, in company, to watch, wide-eyed, those who calmly saunter through life, with the fool's smart aplomb. Out of the old man's closed eyes, the merry bells of Christmas, snowflakes sipping away the bleakness. The waltz of the Eve: warm, smooth skins atremble with a touch. And the silence of the late hour. And the earth-roaring dishevelment winging through the lurch, the grab, the squeeze, the sweating, the panting; while the beggar begs for alms on the frost night air, the gleaming, contented sweat glistens as the sleeping beauty moves softly to desire's gentle touch, opens to its need, cradles its possession, fastens to its rage, strives for its death; the endless, pulsating shudder to the last ebb of joy unshackled. Silence; and sleep in the rapture.

He chuckled, resettling himself more comfortably on the couch.

> 'Ah, sure, God be with the days. God be with the days. And Cafferty's well-grown-up daughter, wherever she is now. And the old Italian who arrived out of the great, wide world beyond the village, at the time I was a wee boy: a multitude of lore and

languages upon his tongue, rekindling the longing for knowledge flogged to crippled ignorance by the cane-happy Canons. The walls of his meek excuse alive with the portraits of civilisations the countries beyond the wee village nourished and flowered. His one room eating-house. A meek excuse to live in an old village in the tralls of nowhere.'

Seeking, perhaps, what those civilisations left out. And when bellowing ignorance drove him brokenly away, his house stood empty: a haunted place to the villagers. Its emptiness so total it stood as a void in the village.

'And sure where are you living now at all, Mulvahy — Ah, in the Empty House.'

Even with Mulvahy living in it the children still called it that. The Empty House. He was missed, even when Mulvahy put the beams of a tripod on the roof and a bell between, and ran the rope down to the window. He was missed. While Mulvahy took to tolling the Angelus and the Mass bells every time he fried a new pot of chips. And the commotion. People crossing themselves and praying with growing but frequent irregularity. One can have too much of a good thing, even religion. And Mulvahy's roaring laughter, and he pealing the tolls of his mockeries into the wind. Before he too went away. And the void stood silent again in the heart of the village. And I found him, years later, broken.

The old man sucked deep on the bottle.

'Isn't it true: the old times are always the best, when you were young, with a fair intelligence and a fair, auld body to shift around in. And the little sorrows, here and there, to relieve the bloody tedium. Heehee.'

He sucked on the bottle again: a hearty gasp and a cuff of the sleeve across his mouth and a sniff of the nose.

'Maybe it's just the bottle, y'be surprised.'

The bottle stood between his legs, an obelisk, while he gazed and rested prone in the chasm's refuge. An unquenchable dimension in eternity, an eternal with dimensions. The sculptured moment, the ending of the act, ending. Alone, now, in the great cities, with the empty night's cobbled squares and their trojan monuments standing, waiting. History staring blindly on.

'Friends, Romans, Countrymen ...'

The old man stopped.

'I must not harrangue ...'

The shining, white-collared moonface above the black soutane came back from the grave.
　'Like him.'
You mustn't, said one, in the heyday of the Empty House, you mustn't preach. You have to do it by entertaining, you see, and that's a curse of a job to give any man.
　The Mass bells tolled from the roof. Chips in fifteen minutes.
　　'A delicate job, that. Getting wits and thoughts sharpened-up: soul and mind rummaging each the other into definition. Great they were to listen to. The wild, learned talk that haunted the formless hypocrisy from its nuance-shrouded guise; and the skilled, pointed words that ran it through. Ah yes. And the talk raging hot on every subject, burnishing it bright and clear, with erudition absorbed and formed to life. Ah indeed!'
The lights were coming up again, and soon the old man would himself die and the resurrected actor declaim his lines again to the thrill-stricken gathering. Strong, hard words bearing the clash of steel wills, the indomitable stride of action briskly apace upon the open, resounding, no-nonsense world.
　　'Ah, y'see, it's all auld art. Nothing more. Marching straight to the grave with trojan words raining a shade of grace on its madness. Life is like that. Jesus. Me swearing that that summed it up. Life is like that. Haahaahaa.'
The old man was getting heated now. God it's incredible how good a man can feel. The lithe steps on the span of time. Life, sweet life, eternity surrounds. March on, just one more step; and the swallowing, inward peace and serenity he craved for all his life. The peace, quiet, and enchantment of the graveyard; with the stupid, the learned, the healthy and the diseased with the rich and the poor.
　　'Ah but there's the rub, hanging on after death. DON'T BURN ME. I might be alive; but muted. Y'know, you see them everywhere.'
The old man peered over the chasm, and quivered a little with a little fear of the burning dread pawing in his stomach. Old now, and to vanish and die soon. But meantime, the penance, for some unknown sin, running the burning dread quivering in his stomach.
　　'Time. The shell of earth's revolving time hatching me back into eternity. But I'll surely be in a troupe. We go in batches through various exits, after the posturing show of a lifetime. But take your time. Only the odd one rushes out before he's called. And

you may be asked to take a bow. That's a sight. The well-trained actors applauding the upstage spectators who ham-acted them.' Isn't it bloody obvious, man, said one under the tolling of the bell, raising his arms in despair that the air didn't shout it for him, and then collapsed, in laugher: Man must act, before he is. His hands went up in the air again. Did you never read zoology. Or glance at the humanities. 'To *Bee* Or Not To *Bee.*'

'Hoho! I loved it. Only children can really love it, as warmly. And all the rest. Summing up life with the grandest of ease and the silk of eloquence. Ah but God me too. And I never knew. Nor the Italian. Nor Mulvahy. We never knew; we were the ones that didn't learn, not even when life kicked it down our throats.'

The old man sat back on the couch.

'Ah! I'll alter the chemicals with another sip on the bottle and a little bit more of me will come out, brighten the old paint again. Ah! God! That's grand now. Aye, sure now, that's fine. A few kind words to meself, now, massaging the old heart with a bit of spirit.'

He muses, and wanders back again into the empty squares, a silent shadow passing the stone monuments and the lights in the subdued, little restaurants along the backstreets: the ear catching the odd murmurs in the silent night, and the tinkles of distant laughter raining on eternity; the sky opening in a fleece of golden clouds and the lash of lightning falling in rage across the native sky. The ending and farewell to the countless previous times when it was youth and a joy unbounded to taste the rage of the elements, safely, and nimbly slip away into the warmth of waiting companionship. Watch elegance modelled across a lounge, poise with a glass, elbow on veneer; glossy, durable, cool, to the first touch, before the sweat of skins warmed each the other. Humanity's need. A screech. In the depth of their nature. And the smiling eyes watching deep for any sign of betrayal of the forthcoming trust.

'These monuments; little figurines of history, standing in the wide spaces of memories. And the old life won't be gone from me 'til either age, distress or happiness, fashions the last one, like the rest, in my mind's eye, and I see myself in the stance of abrupt, open-mouthed death. Never saw a statue like that.'

A tight, brave face came over his fear as he watched for the coming dawn, and the grave ripped from the earth. Hard packed dust, packed harder still, and the dawn's beauty aglow in the sky, the bleakness of winter on the ground as beautiful. Life, in transit, perceiving the elements of nature wrought finely for eternity. And I, the frightened exile: the family waiting, the light above the door.

> 'Again and again, coming back to a village of stone-crofted hutments, noticing the bell gone from the Empty House, the stout beams framing a void against the sky, more telling than when the bell tolled.'

Loneliness, lad, the madness of loneliness was on her — the mourner said as he greeted me — when we found her. There be no hope, you see, she being soaked through with the rain and the cold wind in the night. The mind had gone surely, lad. We found her hugging the mound of your father's grave above on the cliffs. And the night itself would near kill a healthy man with its cold, ne'er mind a slip of an old woman. She screaming and sobbing that he be alive in there.

> 'Aye, you could hear the screaming, hear it tightening into eternity, scalding plain the primitive limp of the village huddled low and fearful against the mountainside.'

I knew what they were waiting for. Would you kiss the corpse of something you loved? Or hold the relic in your arms? Chase eternity with a sob?'

The solemn walk behind another coffin. Another salute to destiny. Another silence in the mind to be endured. Another Gethsemane.

> 'Drinking too much I am. Ought to hobble over and open the window; let fresh air in. Have a gaze and a muse at the Gasworks, and the chimneys stacked around the factories of this city. Maybe catch a whiff of a lost sea breeze. A great trick with me, rubbing the figurines smooth with memories. And sure it soothes me too.'

The old man was happy now, soothing himself as easily as the peasants kneading clay in their hands on the long, cool evenings of summer in his distant, ancient village, sitting on the sloops, musing out over the sea.

> 'Aw, auld sad Longfeller, it's a cold time of the night to be musing, isn't it. And feeling alone and forgotten, like the peasants, away from the mainstream of life, stranded, and facing out at death surely approaching, on the far, far edge of nowhere.'

He felt the toe. It would heal after death. And he crawled on out towards the book; and moved across the span into eternity, eyes agrope at the coming dawn, prone as a sculpture, in abrupt, open-mouthed death lying still on the treadbare carpet, in a shabby room, in a strange city, in another country, the actor, finally, lay mute, banned, finally, from the chasm's refuge.

Marchpast

KAGAN WAS THIRTY YEARS OLD and he had been through one war. Not a world war, nor a European civil war, but yet a war that earned its name. The killing was random, continuous, wanton; and continued after the victorious Indian troops arrived. For eight days of that three week war between India and Pakistan he had eaten no more than half an egg a day. One day the white, one day the yolk. And he had never felt so comfortable, so much at ease, so much alive and ready for all contingencies. Even when he saw for the first time the troops pouring gasoline over the criss-crossed bodies stacked on the roadsides he felt a compassion that was exhilarating, a sense of knowing why, a sense of relief that he could say yes, I saw this horror, I took a part in this. And not vicariously, not by television, by newspapers, by switching channels or turning the page. But directly, as a fulltime job, a job that perversely left him feeling fulfilled, a feeling of doing this dirty work cleaner, with less relish, than anyone else would have; a feeling, ultimately, of having seen mankind's soul, mankind's estate, in the animal kingdom of the world.

The concept of survival, of salvation, meekly disappeared from his mind. When the Indian troops told him he was to be executed a pinge of panic hit him, then vanished, and he turned his back on the troops and waited for the shots. He stood on the roadside and watched the sky knowing this was someone else's way of cleanly doing a dirty job. Or so they would say, if they ever asked for forgiveness.

An Indian officer prodded him with a pistol and said in a perfect British accent: 'The lads hav'n't had too much rest, recently. They're getting a little out of line.' And handed Kagan back his green passport and the neat, string-tied bundle of letters that the troops had confiscated. In the officer's face the firm strength-marks of command, self-command, gave it, almost, a child's pure, serious dignity. Kagan nodded his thanks and understanding. The officer strolled along with him, exchanged a few remarks about the strain and effort, came near to some aspect of the gathered, primeval filthiness that congeals with man into the autonomous, lustful scream of war. And out of respect for each other's guilt they stopped the conversation and walked on silently towards the brilliantly new, luxurious Hotel Palenbang, its windows, roof and walls sprayed with the luminous emblems of the International Red Cross.

Heavy, concentrated bursts of machinegun fire still sounded from around the city. It was not the hysterical, abrupt, crackling sound of combat; it was the war ending as it had begun, with merciless, savage, and arbitrary executions.

On the day he arrived Kagan saw, for the first time, the killing of a man. The troops did it without even the common workmanship of slaughterhousemen killing an animal. Nobody roped the victim; they stood him quivering at the edge of the runway. The Pakistani officer, almost smiling, delightedly proud and flattered, wasted endless minutes upbraiding the firing-party for assuming the wrong positions. He had, somewhere in the world, carried out mock executions on a parade ground, and he thought the wanton reality could have the same text-book, bloodless precision. He was wrong. He could hold no command over the excitement of the troops. While some were held in obedience others giggled nervously, broke the unison of the line, grounded their arms in the confusion, vigorously rubbed their palms against the sides of the trousers, and the officer, trying not to scurry, went along the kneeled and standing lines whipping the offenders with his swagger stick. Kagan never understood the enormity of fear that held the man-prisoner paralysed, and violently trembling, as he stared at his executioners. Finally, after beating the firing-party into a shabby order, and without altering in any way its unskilled stupidity, the officer corrected his uniform, straightened himself, then marched out to the side of the squad. Looking steadfastedly ahead, roaring at the sky, he shouted the order to fire. The prisoner convulted, jerked off the ground; and random, scattered, festive shooting continued from the firing-squad. The officer's facade of propriety broke. He ran and screamed at the troops; and only added the final touch of farmyard savagery. The victim lay, alive, on the ground. The soldiers, in their delight, had aimed at the man's genitals, and now he squirmed, unknown to them under the officer's rage, and clawed at himself. Then a halting, caught, coughing moan came from him. The officer froze, and for the first time authority swelled from him and silenced the group. Nervously he looked around and met Kagan's mocking eyes; and the solution of a proud, arrogant coward smirked across his face. He could avoid the ordeal and pretend he was exercising authority. He walked to Kagan and held out the butt of the pistol. Kagan grabbed it, anxiously, and fired past the officer at the dying man. The shot missed. He walked forward, firing, until the man's head disintegrated into a shower of bone fragments and thick wisps of blood. Then he handed back the gun to the officer and walked away.

The six sailors and two bosuns who had arrived in Dacca, enroute for Chittagong to man the barges sent by the EEC in the wake of the devastation caused by the previous year's endless cyclones, were then driven downtown to the International Hilton. In the diningroom, crowded with news reporters from all over the world, an English journalist told them that India and Pakistan were formally at war. Doing what they had come to do, man the barges and instruct local sailors, would cast them in the role of mercenaries. They would have to refuse and demand repatriation. Kagan watched the two bosuns and his fellow sailors start and exchange glances at the mention of mercenary. And to distract their converging thoughts he asked the journalist about the executions at the airport. These were usual since the partisan attacks had started some weeks previously; and arriving, working class Europeans were usually obliged to witness them. The authorities considered it salutary for all concerned. Working class Europeans arriving at times of war were considered potential mercenaries, and treated roughly.

The group had already been divided into two crews, a bosun and three sailors to each, and now, on the journalist's advice, they physically separated, one group staying with the journalist, the other moving to the far end of the dining hall and into the company of two cameramen from North German TV.

The diningroom was large and windowless, set apart at the right side of the corridor that passed the reception desk from the main door of the hotel. There the corridor branched off as an access to the arcade of shops that surrounded the hotel and they, in turn, served as an outer defence. The street entrances had been blocked off. Everyone had now to pass the military barricade at the main entrance of the hotel. While Kagan and the cameramen were talking, partisans forced the street door of one of the shops and lobbed a bomb directly onto the nest of soldiers at the door. The explosion sounded muted in the diningroom. Hard, impervious, solid, but muted. The tables shook and moved, but then it was over, like an awakening, unaccountably, from a daydream. The experienced recovered themselves from the floor and the novices — the sailors, businessmen and others — sat at their altered tables and stared at each other.

A strained, efficient-looking Pakistani officer came into the room. He looked around for a moment then began selecting witnesses. The group left the room and another battle-hardened soldier, this time a private, stood inside the door, cradled his machinepistol and surveyed the frightened room of war-novices. He leaned back, tentatively, and rested against the wall with a gentleness, an eased touch of relief so spent of energy, interest, emotion; and its lethargy as dangerous to disturb as a wild animal's.

A European, perhaps a seconded civil servant, or a clerk from one of the European banks, tried to dispel the tension.

'Dreadful,' he said, accurately, 'War.' No response came. 'I was a soldier myself once, you know.'

The soldier's eyes closed for a moment. 'Yes, Sahib,' he said, and closed the conversation.

The group of witnesses came back into the room. Most looked pale and shaken. Some had been vomiting and had that sickness plain in their eyes and in the twisted set of their faces. The officer announced that a standard meal would be served; they were then to go to their rooms. It was prohibited to leave the hotel. He had no more information and could render no services; therefore, he would be obliged not to be bothered. The world was aware of the situation and undoubtedly their consulates were aware of the predicament of their nationals and would act accordingly. Already, Canada had placed Air Force transports on standby for the evacuation of foreign non-combatants. That was all. He smiled and sat at a table beside the door. Again the soldier leaned back languidly against the wall; and careful, testing, murmurs of animation started around the room. A British civil servant approached Kagan's table. He introduced himself, in a subdued, quiet voice.

'I'm a British civil servant,' he said to Kagan, 'I'm afraid I can't help you. You're not one of our crowd. Your best bet is the Swiss.' He squeezed Kagan's shoulder in a comradely, affectionate manner. Then he gave the other three sailors individual slips of paper which proclaimed them distressed British seafarers. They were entitled to all aid and assistance from all British personnel and agencies to ensure their repatriation.

Frank, the bosun of the group, tried to protest Kagan's exclusion. But Kagan had never served on a British vessel and was not registered on one now since the barges were lost in a bureaucratic maze. Frank was impressed by the civil servant's language and by its reflection of equality and old boy, chummy, intimacy between two blasé wielders of power: a power that was arbitrary and dangerous because it was so petty. As petty, basically, as a doorman's.

Kagan held his temper and watched Frank's character flick and waggle like a dog's tail to the civil servant's rough, familiar patter.

Frank was about forty years old; an almost small man hardened and fit from constant physical work and a constant appetite for drink and ships' food. And he was untattooed, a sure sign that once he had had aspirations for a berth above that of bosun. He was also an ignorant, bigoted man, sure that he was a good bosun, sure that he had lived a life of asking no favours and sure that that was the way a man, a real man, lived. If a boy didn't grow into a man able to hold his footing on the deck, well, better let him drown, then, if he didn't have it in him. And if a man was foolish enough to lose his footing, well, he deserved what he ought to get, drowning.

Frank mirrored that, called it a philosophy, and explained it at great length to the German cameramen as if he were determined to prove to himself that such a rote learnt repertoire exhibited an intelligent and trained mind incisively summing up some great human predicaments with logical brilliance. The fact of partisans giving up their lives, of the troops of two nations moving into combat, of the mutliated and the dead being cleaned from the hotel foyer; and the worn souls, the untouchable tension of the troopers by the door were details that plain words and a clear head would never tolerate. The Germans listened politely, as if they had never heard this primitive dogma before. And the other two sailors enthusiastically chipped in with comments of the same pseudo masculine, superman tone.

The standard meal was being served and the hum of satisfied conversation from the other tables intermingled in swells of good fellowship and bore the same message. What was needed was a strong man to take a firm grip of the situation. The world was going to hell for want of strong men. And the tea-brokers, the bank clerks, the industrial technicians and advisers, the civil servants, the salesmen, the whole gamut of the dulled, contemporary, peasantry of the cities, lulled themselves with ritual platitudes and shows of common respect for each other's unacknowledged ignorance. Empty, but fashionable, transitory phrases and hollow fashionable words were confidently exchanged as solutions; and as acknowledged displays of intellect. But nowhere was the innate bloodiness of life on earth mentioned. Each knew no reality except his own egoism; and the history and nature of man were mirrors that showed no more than the petty attributes of each individual. They could do no more then than use the plodding examples of their work to resolve the conflicts in man that lead to war. From nine to five and the virtues and contentment of steady, regular work, from using the dry seasons to prepare for the wet, to doing things as they ought to be done, as they've always been done, to a firm footing to a faulty footing, to a strong, personable man taking a firm grip on the situation.

It was their callous lameness of thought that revolted Kagan. Their lameness of thought, its arrogance, the ease with which they unblushingly metamorphosed their parochialisms and bigotries as solutions so blind to reality, man's nature and history, and so very much the essence of conflict that even their conceits of solutions bred and multiplied the essence of further conflicts.

Kagan left the table, walked across to the Pakistani officer, introduced himself, briefly explained why he was in East Pakistan, and asked for permission to carry on to Chittagong.

The officer was chewing resignedly at the distasteful, European-styled food. He looked up and smiled, very lightly, very knowingly.

'Chittagong is a long way from the Indian bomber bases, my friend, but it isn't out of range. They'll fly across the Gulf.'

Kagan immediately admired the man, and smiled back.

'I still want to go there. I can make myself useful.' He held up the keyplaque and showed the room number, then nodded and left.

It was bravado, mere childish bravado, and whatever its cause, had the same lack of control, the same ineptness of command as the firing-squad officer at the airport. And the same inverted cowardice, without its justification. Kagan's soldiers were unwarranted impulses forever likely to break rank and leave him usurped from the kind of person he wanted to be, leave him obliged to defend the kind of person he was, at the mercy of an impulse, or condemn himself.

This common dilemma lamed Kagan's life. It came with the growing awareness of the vain strutting and affectation of the teachers in his small world of school life, and with the gathering, hardening suspicions that these men were confined and limited to conjugating the set, approved texts; and could do no more, could not advance, but juggled endlessly with small knowledge and pleased themselves. The fretfulness of wasting years on their redundant, used, blueprints of knowledge, blueprints for foundations that would never be built, and never built upon, and the fretfulness of spying through their antics to their hypocrisy frightened Kagan. Frightened and fretful he squirmed under their tutelage, revolted by impulse, and discovered that learning, unlike conduct, was not treated seriously. Learning was no more than a menial servant in the pursuit of the vanities of life, and conduct was its master.

It was a day the ex-pupils and the teachers playfully but too accurately called old boys' day, the day the foremen artisans, the office clerks, the odd lawyer and the clerics wandered about the school condescending to the pupils and to each other. They wore their professions as surely as if they were military uniforms; and displayed what women and wealth and other vanities they had secured as if they were campaign ribbons. And when the strangely vying, costumed-dressed females nested into private, perfumed groups, the old boys guffawed to bicycle-shed stories of women and showed a crudity as vast as the pupils' as arms flashed watches for the name, lapels thumbed and shoes angled with the conversation in a sad, disillusioning spectacle of strange savages meeting and admiring each others' tinsel and bead. But they served their purpose, and very quickly wagged their characters to the sway of the leader, and joking jocularity nosed its way in and out of the laughing clusters.

The wounds and suffering behind the ribbons were invisible. The bravery it needed for these men to put a smile over sadness and disappointment unknowable to him, and he saw no more than a normal trite, social gathering. The next day he lay in bed. And the day after he cycled about the city, for a while, then ran out of activities to amuse himself with, and cycled along the docks to kill time. Within a day the details were arranged, and he signed ship's articles, went on board, and waited for the vessel to sail and bring him release.

That had been fifteen years earlier and he was still surprised that the bravado was so ungovernably childish, that the self-condemnation was still not by admittance and retraction but by commission. The impulse ruled, and he followed, limping.

His room was on the fourth floor of the hotel. At each landing he was stopped and searched, automatically and without questioning. The room was large, sumptuous, cool. And he had surrendered it merely to express his contempt, knew no other way to express his contempt but to forever surrender what little he ever had, and doing it not blindly, and not with vision, but as if mesmerised.

He sat, sensing the spell, knowing that at every opportunity he committed unreasoned, thoughtless damage to his life, prodded at fate in petty ways, then passively left the running of his life to the passing nights and days, left himself a careless hostage to time, but dared not force the hand to a premature conclusion, dared not openly desert the unused days and nights for the sanctuary of suicide. The ersatz suicides acceptable to society, the fanaticisms for and against political and religious creeds, did not identify with his existence and could not release it into something more meaningful. Kagan was the animal of his body, and no more. And he knew it.

He looked at the sum of his possessions lying in the suitcase. There was no great gamble in going on to Chittagong, there was nothing to lose, but it might bluff fate, might make it show its hand. Europe already hinted that time was altering its bizarre run of prosperous days. Ships lay idle in the ports and trampship sailors lay about, workless, in the harbour dosshouses. Even those who found work found that a dourness, a caution, had crept over it; and they trod warily, irked by the burden of what had once been a casual existence of signing-on and signing-off ships: when it was accepted that you signed aboard broke, worked off the contract, then went ashore and blew a year's pay, or half a year's pay, in a couple of weeks. A little more, a little less. Then you signed-on again, did your work and asked no questions, comforted every sorrow with the dream of the day the contract would end; and you could walk down the gangway, free and rich; and do exactly as you pleased when you pleased. Until the money ran out, as it always did, a day sooner than you'd expected, and you were beached for a cigarette, a beer, a meal, a bed, for that day, or two. And then relieved and glad to sign-on again. It was an endless carousel, bringing you nowhere; and your most silent, sacred wish was to fall off before the music stopped, before age beached you into the dour slumps of men stranded about the harbour.

He was half-awake, dreaming of the past and its weakened demands on the future, when the officer rapped on the door and came in.

'Ready?'

'Yes.'

They stood and looked at each other, silently, as if they were brothers about to part forever. And they both knew it. There were no barriers between them; not even the parochial barriers of cultures, of different skin-colours. Each knew how the other had judged life, each knew they had reached the same conclusion. And they shared the regret of parting as strangers.

The street was quiet. It was the first night of war and the soldiers spoke in whispers and occasionally glanced at the sky. The air of reverence, mixed with doubt and non-belief in the coming of this ancient God, imposed an uneasy compliance by its grandeur. The officer spoke to a soldier, and his voice seemed to travel along the walls of the street like a disrespectful, unsettling, murmur. An unlit jeep, its engine humming reassuringly, emerged from the shadows. Kagan and the officer shook hands. The moment held; and they stood, without any movement, and stonily stared at each other, their eyes smiling, savouring and enjoying the irony that bonded them in their contempt for the strong old boys of diningrooms, the old men of life, who put down their foot and stamped for Daddy! Daddy!! The officer turned, without a word, and walked away.

At the airport a C-47 transport, cargo-rigged, and painted a drab, jungle-daub camouflage on top, and plain blue on the underbelly and under the wings, was loading dis-spirited shuffling soldiers. On board they were praying. Standing, and praying out loud, holding their unslung rifles with one hand, hanging to an overhead bar with the other, they prayed solemnly and continuously, each man saying a different prayer to his neighbour's, or a different part of the same prayer. Against the roar of the engines on take-off, throughout the thuds and bumps and sickening drops of the Dakota flying low across country, the high-pitched, bald, unmitigated praying continued its mournful cry. As the aircraft slowed after touchdown the praying ceased, with relief, and the prayerful gave themselves over to renewed bravery and to spitting on the floor.

It was irksome, then, to watch them; to be in their presence. These were the journeymen of war, descended from warriors that once were shaved and painted, and as animally glorious as leopards. Now they were uncouth, lethargic, ignorant, and caged in uniforms, their glorious, animal tribalism reduced to strips of colours on their sleeves. Herded naked and praying onto transports, it would have been slavery; but the uniforms made it something else, and covered the deceit.

And Kagan began to feel a total indifference to all that went on around him. It was the only escape left. The indifference that would have saved him from leaving school too young, from a life of sacred, silent wishes, from walking across to the officer in the diningroom at Dacca, the reluctant but heavy indifference that should have been his first option came now with the force of a prodigal. Whatever might happen to these praying soldiers, whatever might happen to anyone, did not matter. The world was already defeated, and he had been born into its routed army. The sacred, silent wish had not been fulfilled.

While his papers were being checked in the airport terminal the first air-raid began. The sun had barely risen, and the bombers seemed to come directly out of it. Huge, massively huge, swooping firmly and priestlike across the brightening day. They came without warning, the radar blind to them by their path out of the sun, the hungry power of engines, the ceaseless poundings of the rockets, time after time as the planes curved away and swung back, almost an entire squadron in turns of threes, and bombed the airport to rubble. Then they finally rose, like startled vultures from a carcase, and disappeared into the sky. Then, and only then it seemed, the wounded began their cries; and the spared moved and crawled and checked their bodies. An endless, blinding amount of dust choked the broken buildings. Odd figures moved about, ghostly and leaderless. Small groups of survivors gathered together with heart-broken rage, incomprehension, and eddies of hysteria mingling through the dust, from group to group. Then the first delayed-action bomb exploded, and an audible scream of terror hit against the walls. The buildings were cleared, a water-ration issued, and teams organised into search parties to re-enter the ominous, dead ruins. Occasionally, shots rang out in acts of mercy.

Rickshaws began to ferry away the dead and wounded. And no one, in any capacity, gave a damn for the stranded sailor sitting amid the confusion, sitting placidly sad and withdrawn, and awaiting nothing.

Unshamed, declared cowardice; mean, selfish panic that had endangered others in its fury for survival, and the most brazen fear began to cower in those now inflamed and alert with released bravery, arrogance, and a rag of potency. A soldier, drunk with near hysteria, pushed Kagan, grunted and gesticulated, holding himself in a Tamburlaine posture of pride and fearlessness. Very soon roars and demands would not satisfy his cravings for subjugating power. Nothing would, but the handling of a machine-pistol as it plucked open bodies would relieve it, and he'd grow tough and contented with that. For these soldiers, forever deviated from maturity by the ersatz suicide of their elders, war and its armaments were substitutes, then proof, of instantly demonstrable, sure manhood. It was all they would ever know, like their elders, of passion.

He pushed Kagan towards a rickshaw and shouted orders to the driver. During the ride through the city the old, worn driver kept glancing back to smile at Kagan, and Kagan twitched his features in response.

At the Palenbang Hotel, for want of money, he gave the old man a new looking shirt from his suitcase. The old man smiled happily, then guided Kagan past the military guardpost to the door of the hotel. He then tried to relay the soldier's orders and establish Kagan's bona fides to the hotel clerk. The clerk looked at Kagan and admitted him, but needlessly pushed the old man away. The old man bowed meekly while still off balance, making no attempt to veil this humiliation, and walked uncomplainingly away. He didn't even sigh, just bowed and walked away, long accustomed to humiliation, but no longer interested in acknowledging it otherwise.

The dispossessed had given their consent; they had said no, they refused to yield up their minds and hopes to the commands of their rulers. An animal of rebellion had awoken with a million arms, and the cutting swords of the ruler extended their reach. And they reached first into those strange places called the mission-schools. And killed.

In the Palenbang Hotel sheltered missionaries and clerks dominated the foyer. They had lists and names and occupied themselves in an exchange of circular activity, and the blinkered zeal of suicides. Whatever had turned so many into partisans that a war had resulted was unknown to these men. They named the unknown a lack of their professionalism, of christianity, and carried on with their activity.

A minister of some religion explained to Kagan that the military had confiscated the hotel's provisions. They only had eggs left and had intended a jolly good time of scrambled, boiled, poached, what-have-you eggs. But an odd man out, a young Englishman with whom Kagan would be paired, had persuaded them that the war might last longer than a couple of days. All were healthy and, accustomed to eating well, were well-stocked. Hence the rationing would be as severe as possible, half an egg each per day, until the situation became clear. The day's ration would be issued each evening. He smiled at Kagan: jolly good fun, hey!

Kagan was irked by the frivolity, but refused to show it. He had a feeling it might please the man, and he knew he lacked the gift of making his displeasure socially acceptable, but daunting. The young Englishman had a casual, unconcerned confidence; and a quick, brutal reply.

'Yes. Jolly God. Now rub your hands and ask him to turn the other cheek. Or perhaps the man isn't as christian as you.'

The cleric's hands were spread in a manner of contentment across an extended stomach. He swayed back and forth, benign. 'Now, now,' he said, 'Now, now.'

Yet the visible tinge of learning and culture, and of a demoted self-interest in the young Englishman's attitude, held the clerics constrained in their approach to him. Kagan was excluded from their dominance and authority; and left unheeded, a tactic they feared to use with the young Englishman. Instead they caught at every word as if to reconcile it to their various dogmas, fearful that they might unwittingly expose themselves as heretics. They were uneasy in the presence of such a threat, and not wise enough to know that Kagan could see it.

He asked Kagan for details of the raid on the airport, then predicted, correctly, that the next raid would come at noon and the following one at sunset. And in a pleasant manner explained the blocking effect of the sun on radar tracking stations. He was quite wrong, but that served to disarm any hidden suspicions and allowed a greater range of charm in his account to the enraptured missionaries.

'Oh!' said one, hopping delightedly to the bait, 'Were you in the RAF?'

'Never. I have a distaste for uniforms,' he answered, and added a remark that cut too deep, 'They have the neat vulgarity of clerics.'

'And just what do you do for a living?' Instantly demanded another.

The young Englishman smiled, 'Oh!' he said, and let the word hang for a moment in the silence, 'I'm a sailor. Yes, just like Kagan. I'm a stranded sailor.'

That night he gave his share of the egg to Kagan. Discreetly, while the others took their shares with insistent demand under a show of scampering, boyish caperings, he gave his ration away. And in return Kagan invited him to share the now-valueless, duty-free bottle of whisky.

They went to the roof and sipped contentedly from the bottle, without exchanging any pretence of conversation, and watched the artless array of colours in the mysterious, saddening sky. They were drunk, but still awake, still silent, when the morning air-raid started. Its moronic noise became deafening, and the raid took on an eerily silent quality as it displayed the primitive application of primitive principles only as noise in the great hollowness of the universe, the waves ringing forever throughout the transformations of energy into life, and consciousness. A crude experiment of life taking life as savages devouring their victims' brains. Its object so purposeless; the billowing waves of fire and smoke so much the blood and bodies of a laboratory slaughterhouse smeared between earth and sky. The species doctoring itself, clawing at itself, the clawed part clawing back, the self-mutilation an obscenity of its reasoning; but an exact and artful frieze of the species.

Kagan took the last of the bottle and they started for their rooms; and in an angry, provoking manner shouldered and clumsily bumped into the clerics racing in awe to view the carnage. It was the nearest any ever came to communicating, to acknowledging the wound of interdependence, to forgiving themselves for being less than their vanity.

The first days of war passed. Very rapidly the light-headed giddiness of hunger spread throughout the hotel. Water had to be boiled and let cool before drinking. Day by day they boiled and drank litre after litre of the insipid, deadened water; listened morosely to the air-raids and the coffin-like thuds of small arms fire as more buildings, streets and areas fell into the partisans' control. Each night the ration of eggs was boiled, shelled, distributed; but already the men would have separated from their ration-partners and formed parallel lines awaiting the yellow or the white. Kagan and the young Englishman, more deferred to, consulted, and obliged with petty favours, played a game of postponing the ration, eating it casually and lightly, throwing bits away, at all costs refusing it dominance over them and denying its belittling importance.

The days seemed to slow down, the noise of war more and more unbearable, the deadened water sickening, the ridiculous half-egg more maddening; and even the staunchest of the clerics more susceptible to the callousness of the young Englishman's remarks. The tone of his being, his presence, seemed to remind them of what they were not, and this was the essence of his attraction and his power. A reluctant prefect, no more, but the macled radiance dazzled them. It blinded them when they played chess with him to pass the time; turned the game into a visible extention of their assumptions as they accepted mistakes for strategy, panicked, and blundered in reply. They did this as naturally as they blundered in their condescension to Kagan. And in each case, after each humiliation, they retreated to the incubating warmth of their class milieu. There they were safe. Not even the gripping, dizzying hunger, nor the noise and the fear of war could alter their perspective. They turned their backs on the terror and huddled closer; not afraid when they were not alone.

When they grouped to watch Kagan and the young Englishman play chess they submerged, sometimes almost lost, the external shows that defined them. The gambits, the poisoning of squares and pieces, the balanced probes that emerged from the set of the game and seized a magic of art across the board enraptured them. They became alert, receptive, understanding. A less crude, a more developed art, would have freed them, would have revealed the universal laws that they had banished with symbols, and superstitions; and all else that defined them. A piece on the chessboard was moved and they murmured in a rush of enthusiasm. In a way they understood the young Englishman groaned at them; and they submitted to silence.

' "To build a universe with farthing balls." ' he quoted, and bowed his head back to the game.

The spell was broken, the chance to communicate at a level deeper than external shows lost; perceived reality again asserted itself as truth, and the bond of communication dismissed as a groaning fantasy.

The game was soon over and Kagan wandered about the hotel, checking first that his name stayed scrawled off the neat, handwritten lists of residents, and that no new lists had been added to the ones already posted about the walls of the hotel. Lists were an obsession of the clerics, with nationalities and passport numbers displayed alongside the alphabetically arranged names. This was the formalisation of their plight. They were hungry and destitute, but now respectable; aid could be asked for, almost demanded, as a right due to humanity. But the lists had no more power than tombstones. Each resembled nothing so much as a plaque over a mass-grave, and Kagan was unwilling to see his name inscribed.

A group of bored soldiers lounged by the main door. Kagan smiled and went through a sign-language introduction of aircraft diving, fingers of anti-aircraft fire shooting into the sky, and aircraft pitching and tumbling to the earth. The soldiers copied. They knew already they were on the losing side, and had sympathy for other losers. Kagan drew the side of his hand across his stomach, and grimaced in hunger. One of the soldiers pointed to the trucks in the courtyard, tapped his cigarette and ground the ash with disgust. Kagan drew a square in the air and the soldier copied, a bigger square, a drum. He tapped the backs of his fingers and rolled his hands, dozens of drums. Kagan gestured an offer of exchange: shirt for drum, and the soldier agreed. He passed by the barricade to the trucks and came back with a large, Red Cross can: powdered eggs; and pictorial instructions stamped into the metal. Another shirt-for-can swop was arranged, but Kagan pointed to the egg symbol and shook his head in refusal; and the soldier smiled and nodded. The young Englishman came to participate and, after him, trails of clerics. The joy of food, its relief and abundance available in return for the tinsel of pens, for the black, silver-clasped notebooks and the other worthless oddities of pockets, brought the soldiers and clerics into a melee of loot and booty, shouting and pushing with childish delight. Cans of powdered potatoes, eggs, soups, spinach, rice, even cans of vitamin powder were eagerly exchanged by the troops for the sham sparkle of cuff-links and tie-pins. Inexorably, with the conniving greed of both sides turning hysterical, the price began to rise. Touches of animosity and contempt passed back and forth with the bartering. Hints of cheating, of exploiting the weak, passed the language-barrier with smirks and gestures to comrades, and offended retreats from the trading. The soldiers drifted back to the main door and re-traded the tinsel and novelties among themselves, regaining their good humour and spirit. Kagan, to keep open the access to them, traded his last shirts for a bottle of arrack. The seller was the soldier who had traded the first tin, and he shared Kagan's disappointment at the surly greed that had poisoned the other exchanges.

In the kitchens the clerics timorously followed the symbolic instructions on the cans. The result was slop. More powder was measured out and shaken into the mess. Slowly, even more slowly still, the mess congealed into unbeaten, soggy powder. It was unbearable to watch so many men, ruptured from their polished grooves where they shone and basked in the reflected glow of routine, try now to cope with the most simple instructions. And then they ate the slop, reluctantly, allowing hunger to spur them.

It wasn't difficult to make a more pleasing, a more satisfying, meal. But the rush of food into the body, after days of starvation, hurt. Breathing became heavy and difficult, and the stomach kept threatening to cramp. Their eyes blinded rapidly, as if about to weep, and all the anxieties of hunger disappeared in the rush of nourished, delighted blood around the stimulated body.

The soldier had watched Kagan and the young Englishman turn the powder into thin soup, then knead it with flour from a different tin until it became potato diced with vegetables, and a rainbow-coloured feast toasted golden and healthy. In return he gestured towards the arrack, towards the roof, and nodded wisely. There was the place to get quietly drunk, and leave the body to work its own magic in sleep; and a riot of drunken dreams.

The arrack was sweet, slippery. It lay and burnt in the throat, and offered no compensation for enduring the charred rivulets of heat. Then the numbing drunkenness spread like a death over the body, and an oblivion of peace and serenity; the reasoning engine pacified and extinguished, for the bliss of sleep.

Morning came, and they awoke cold and shivering on the roof. The young soldier was gone. Gunshots, and screams and shouts as loud as gunshots, came from the streets below in breaks of panic as feet scurried from one place to another. Grown men in uniforms squatted, fired at each other, then ran from place to place, dodged each other, and shouted, earnestly, and squirmed hard against the ground for cover. Without brilliance, skill, or purpose, without the hushed elegance of stalking animals moving through the clean, jungle air, the spitting journeymen of war stumbled across the ground and snarled, as helplessly, as incongruously, as a platoon of monkeys raging for the favours of a wooden-faced, hideous female.

Kagan looked to the young Englishman, but the young Englishman stared into space and listened to the gunfire. It went on in an endless, irritating spasm, without hope of resolution, the recoil of each burst of fire lulling as a threat, never a reprieve. In the silence Kagan lobbed the empty bottle over the parapet. For a moment it sailed quietly towards the ground, then a barrage of fire from several points exploded through the air, feet scampered again, and voices cried. Kagan and the young Englishman watched each other. It was of no moment; no man had died, no man was down there waging war; merely animals contesting the strength of their vanities, a frightening spectacle, but no more so than meeting any other familiar yet so strangely different animal. Their existence had a reason, as surely as Kagan's fear; but in an altered context, some other and narrower band of consciousness. The fear was in Kagan because he understood they could never communicate, despite all outward shows.

The young Englishmen touched his elbow and they turned to crawl from the roof. Going down the stairs they met two European Red Cross workers searching the hotel. The authorities had conceded the presence of missionaries and clerics in the hotel and had allowed the Red Cross in to paint their signs, distribute food, and arrange a safe evacuation. A vessel stranded in the port now had permission to sail; and would be guided through the first minefield by Pakistani pilots and through the second by Indian warships.

The news had set the missionaries noisy with excitement. More lists were being compiled and duplicated. Laughter and goodfellowship swamped all their activities, and they never heard the odd, sustained bursts of fire from the gunbattle outside. The soldier who had sold the arrack stood by the main door. Kagan waved to him and gestured towards the roof. The soldier frowned, bewildered, and smiled to show it. Kagan fired an imaginary pistol and drew a finger across his throat. Immediately the soldier brightened and waved that he understood, then repeated the gesture of the finger drawn across the throat, spoke to his comrades and led them, scattering missionaries haphazardly about the lobby, in a military run across to the stairs and onwards to the roof. Kagan realised the mistake, then relaxed, assured that the unskilled butchery would at least cease. The noise of the gunfire in the streets dimmed, then turned into a concentrated roar coming from just one point. Then it coughed haltingly for some moments, and died.

The cheerful soldiers came running back down the stairs, and smiled in triumph. Either they were all strangely innovate in an identical way or they had, somehow and somewhere in this world, learned the expected response; or else they had no choice. They were now behaving in the expected way to the Red Cross lady who politely questioned them. They hushed, and sullenly answered, mumbled, and showed flashes of rebellion. She questioned more, and they became more embarrassed, more willing to express nervous hostility, yet regretting the event only for the confrontation it now caused with uncomfortable, unnamed feelings. The Red Cross lady prodded some more, then turned to Kagan.

'He says you told him to fire from the roof,' she said.

'He may have believed that. But I didn't.' Kagan answered.

'On the contrary,' a cleric said, 'You did. I saw you pretend to fire a pistol and gesture towards the roof.'

The young Englishman laughed, and vulnerability spread across the faces of the clerics, rippled there for a moment, mocked before the insult was said, and made the saying redundant.

'You chaps hav'n't been so successful in your mission here, have you?' he asked, 'That a mere nod will send the natives into battle.'

The Red Cross lady sighed, plainly showing her weariness for the immutable childishness that she had to endure from the daily people of her life. She spoke once more in Bengali to the soldiers, then turned to the waiting Europeans.

'The hotel is extraterritorial property granted to the Swiss Consulate. Please remember that.'

Kagan nodded, then checked the gesture, and the lady smiled as if meeting a kindred spirit.

'May I speak to you privately?' she asked.

Kagan smiled back and nodded again, in the same fashion, and followed the lady to the hotel manager's office.

'One of the lists I have here says you've come to this area to work. Is that correct?'

'I'd rather work here than go back to Europe.' He showed her the contract, its paragraph of escape clauses, and explained the nightmare of arriving back penniless in Europe in the middle of winter.

'My concern is to save you from this situation only,' she explained, 'That soldier thinks he is your friend, but if he mentions you in his report I think your safety will be endangered. I tried to explain to him. Therefore I want you to go to another Red Cross station. You may work there if you wish.'

He smiled at her. Her determined calmness, and the honest unwillingness to allow a feeling of kinship to disturb her pragmatism with concern for the everyday woes of his life, stemmed his enthusiasm and gave a quiet maturity, an appreciation, for the ease that could be taken despite the war, the casual acceptance of life until death came and then, too, the casual acceptance of death. Excitement over either was out of place.

She gave him a map of the city with the route from the hotel to the harbour Red Cross station indicated, and a letter of authorisation. Breaking the twenty-four-hour curfew would be dangerous, but the risk could be taken after the noon air-raid when the wounded straggled through the streets in search of first-aid centres. Military and partisans allowed for this traffic in their own anxiety to limit and assuage the barbarity of the fighting. Only then could the enemies lie side by side, wounded, and freed by shock from their adopted patterns of hate.

Outside, Kagan and the young Englishman walked across the foyer to the military guardpost and sat down with the troops. The pre-air-raid hush, and its silent, frightened deals with fate, began. Ahead of its own noise the first aircraft dipped from the sky, straightened. The wings jolted, two rockets dropped in the silence, then accelerated as the blinding scream of noise hit the city, and dived to their targets. The bombers came next with huge open bellies tumbling out black ribbons that grew and draped, casually, as shrouds of death across the burning city, each bomb marking its grave with a blossoming pall of smoke. And in the air, the fighter-pilots stubbornly played with their airplanes, more safe than most of the people on the innocent land below.

Before the raid ended, Kagan and the young Englishman shook hands and exchanged smiles with the troopers, crossed the forecourt to the main barricade, and slipped past its unmanned presence onto the street. For want of shelter the soldiers were well-spaced along the road, increasing the chance that one would die, but reducing to almost zero the possibility that all would die. Each man crouched on the ground with his hands over his head, and none heard or cared as Kagan and the young Englishman paced down the deadened streets.

The young Englishman pressed himself against the wall of the abandoned school-house that now served as the harbour Red Cross station. Kagan pounded on the door, and an English voice answered. Kagan replied. The door opened cautiously and Kagan handed in the letter of authorisation. A small, old man, looking shrunk and emaciated in a string vest and shorts, opened the door wide and eagerly greeted Kagan. The noise of the raid made normal formalities impossible, but the doctor's happiness precluded them with its solitary joy. Smilingly Kagan took back the letter and threw it dismissingly onto the street, waving away its usefulness to them. The doctor thoughtlessly agreed, and Kagan closed the door on one more rare friend lost to the casual rush of circumstance. Whatever group they belonged to moved according to its law, and in it their antics of independence moved freely and proud and subjected to its government. And no one willed the regret of parting, nor the making of bosom friends.

While the young Englishman was blinked out of existence with a map, a letter, and his hunger to serve his needs, the doctor showed Kagan about the makeshift hospital and explained the routine of treating all, but allowing neither partisan nor soldier to stay. Patrols from either side occasionally searched, and randomly shot their wounded enemies. And so on blankets on the floor of the main ward lay the women, from children to the very old, thin and fat, the ugly and beautiful all reduced now to the blandness of a common fate. Neither lust nor hate could account for their condition, but an indomitable potency of each in the raping soldier's mind, the wide-eyed, obedient, jerking motions of his body striving for his release from his own nature.

The women appeared strangely equal. Although the mobile washed and cooked for the others, no leader, no mother-figure, ever emerged. And Kagan followed the doctor's instructions never to let them see the spoonfuls of sedative powder he mixed with the Red Cross cocoa. But their love for the cocoa was undisguised, and weak smiles often lit their faces as they took the mugs, and sipped, placid and humourlessly content in their private worlds. Occasionally one would offer him a sip from the other side of the mug, to share her joy, and he would sip and smile gratefully back; each time more sincere. And it helped master the task of dragging the still warm dead out onto the streets where the criss-crossed corpses sagged as the rats nimbly and greedily ate. Fat and relentlessly eating, they allowed themselves to be soaked as the gasoline was poured over the bodies and the flames jumped from the match and paralysed them with pain. And some would tear themselves away burning like torches, and abruptly stop and fall dying only metres from the pyre. But no pyre burned enough to reduce the bodies to ash, and long before the flames died down the gnawing of the rats would mingle with the smoke.

Slowly, and satisfyingly, the energy of the idle days was used up. And at moments in the day and night he would find all the tasks done, and an oasis of respite replenishing his care and energy for life. It meant nothing if this was the only way to learn, or else it meant that rats learned in the same way. But it provided nourishment for the mind, and a strong sense of community with victims, a strong desire to identify the cause of their state beyond its mere implements and weapons. Helping these, the wounded and the maimed, taught Kagan that he was not a completed man, like the young Englishman; but it showed him also that he was undamaged and whole.

Each evening, by common consent, whispering groups of frightened civilians broke the curfew and crept down the streets like shadows. And behind the shadows came the petty blackmarket racketeers willing to trade handfuls of rice for tins of Red Cross powdered food; and for a higher price, pieces of strange, stringy meat. Food was distributed according to the names on the school's rollcall books, and each child was entitled to five rations for parents and one brother and sister. The overlap of children enrolled from one family covered the certainty of families being larger than five, so that a surplus of food was distributed and accounted for relatives and grandparents. Kagan brought down the rations from the padlocked storeroom and set them by the open street door. After that the women, with their resigned acceptance of the needs and oddities of the neighbourhood, gave out the food, and divided the remainder between the lone adults.

A very pleasant gentleness existed in these moments. After the door was closed and the women went to settle for the night, Kagan sat with a bottle of arrack and waited. If work was light the doctor joined him, glad of the company of at least a European to whom his contempt for the native people could be expressed as a just man's disappointment. The arrack helped him, and brought rosy visions of his life as a young man when he first arrived in Asia. It was long before the other war, the other war back home, that sad, sweet time of comradeship. Now the tide of colonialism had ebbed, and he was stranded in a foreign, hostile nation. The era of values he had been reared in had passed, and Europe and its servantless ways was no longer his home. Asia more resembled the old Europe, but the people didn't fit. Arrack had become his last companion and he never hoped, for very long, for much more.

The nights and days passed. The state of war was now the accepted state, the authority for its existence never questioned, its bloodletting a direct function and definition of man, until it seemed that death had merely increased its daily toll by other means.

The doctor worked and drank, and took his sleep curled up on a cot. Silently, in the wide, unearthly silences that lay between deaths, his body shrunk to a child's as he lay alone and let odd mumblings slip past his guard and die in the spittle of exhaustion scumming at the side of his mouth. He respected the strain, eager to accept its need, its purpose, as giving him a leverage, a use, in life. In the way the women became trained and passive by rape and sedatives, and dogwise swayed to lean in any way for a continuance of the hospital's grace, in the same broken, wrongly re-knit way, the doctor was in awe of war, and felt enriched and ennobled by suffering its presence. And no ennobling contempt for war's betrayal of humanity ever touched him. The challenge was all, and a man's work. And to it he brought notions of prosperity as labour and production was destroyed and created need and demand and work for another generation rebuilding the old. The simplicity of merely throwing all into the sea had no magic for him, unlike the beauty of the randomness of war. It was the highest he could reach towards a poetry, a romance, of life.

Never knowing why, never realising the charade he played, the doctor hid his life behind his profession; and there it atrophied, an ersatz suicide buried in the sand. Yet he had no urge, no vocation, no talent and so no writ other than a diploma to practice his profession. Its purpose to others was incidental, and beneath the purpose it served to him. When he broke down, crumbling on his side on the floor, eyes wide and transfixed on some unknown demon or god, Kagan carried him to the cot upstairs, wrapped him in blankets, and hugged him as a child.

It was the tenth day of Kagan's work at the station. Indian troops had taken a nearby village, Cox's Bazaar, and marker shells had begun, clumsily groping for their targets, to fall on Chittagong. They came in a steady, invincible march, thudding agony and speechless horror into the city with slow relentlessness, marked the city as a coffin and nailed each shell fast to siege the living remnants inside. Air-raids can be endured because they end; shelling exposes the time left to live, determines its ever decreasing span as sullenly as a labouring, stilted hate, then postpones its ponderous judgement and kills in another place, ruptures another's span, and promises its deceit will whip and change until all life is put to death.

The doctor's mind closed against the promise. Kagan tried to follow the prescription in the first-aid book and provided as much warmth and seclusion as possible. But the necessary quietness only existed in strained, fretful spasms; and measures of re-assurance and measures of drugs brought no rays of hope. No one would take a message to another station. The streets now reeked of carnage, and death hovered, as in a plague, in every breath drawn.

For want of the doctor's skill the women were left dampened with sedatives, and the wounded sat and lay about the place and nodded on morphine. For lack of elementary skill with a scalpel, for lack of its training confidence in facing ripped bodies and their mysterious insides, the willing Kagan was helpless. Within a day the aspect of a charnel house touched the station as perceptibly as a vulture's shadow. And the last hope lay at the end of a journey through the opening of the streets.

Then he was walking in the street, in despair and panic, blindly holding the Red Cross flag, walking as if crossing unknown land on a dark, moonless night, each step a slow achievement, each breath struggled for, and released in a tremor of fear, each keen noise he heard a ghoulish harbinger of following death.

The missionaries, the clerics and the clerks, were still at the Palenbang. Day by day their rescue convoy had been postponed. And still they were compiling lists of farthing balls. The Red Cross lady still administered, unperturbed by folly. Indian troops had taken the airport and the rim of the city. Soon Canadian airforce transports would land on the reconstructed runways and bring scores of trained volunteers, ferry back jubilant refugees. An endless war would commit its last deceit, and end. And soon the sweetness of selected memories would fall as a shroud over its sacred name.

The bubble of energy and intelligence never subsided in the Red Cross lady as she listened to Kagan and jotted notes, asked questions, nodded in surmise of forthcoming explanations, and explained that even the most copious resources disappeared into trickles in the ever-growing number of casualties. He was still needed at the harbour station. Dampeners in the cocoa, morphine and commonsense, would have to serve for want of better. He would have to go back.

In the foyer the missionaries crowded around. They had duplicated their lists and letters, in case of accident, and since the harbour station might be liberated from the war first the neatly tied and labelled bundle was handed to Kagan. He took it, and they stood and thanked him in the stilted and almost acted way of formality. He passed through the doorway and across the courtyard. At the unmanned barricade, webbings, arms and uniforms lay abandoned on the ground.

The first street was silent and empty, a landscape of scarred deserted building out of place and altered with the aspect of sudden, benumbing fear. From the harbour the dim, interred sounds of shelling drifted along the walls. Kagan, in the middle of the road, moved out to cross the top of an intersecting street. An impatient, angry shout roared a warning. Kagan stood still and raised his hands over his head, feeling the cloth of the Red Cross flag drape and hide the emblem in folds along the flagstaff. Two tanks, sheltering a swarm of soldiers on their flanks, moved side by side up the street. They halted, inscrutable, dim, questioning; then ungainly lurched forward again and recommenced their slow, careful tread into the unknown. In overlapping patterns soldiers broke in twos from the swarm to search the houses on either side of the street. Occasionally a pitched, imploring scream sounded in terror until the impervious command of a machinepistol brought unearthly silence again. Scouting soldiers overtook the tanks and examined the intersection. They gestured to Kagan to turn around, and again, then beckoned him in to the side of the street. The tanks moved out and around the corner in the direction of the Palenbang. A soldier searched Kagan then passed on. A group from the following soldiers formed about the specimen of Kagan. They were ebullient, almost frothing, with the transcendental glory of their power and righteousness bracing their shrill voices into hard confidence, their movements into flowing, elegant strength. The leader held his machinepistol as a bar, and raised it into the air. Triumphantly the others did likewise, and copied the shout of victory. Kagan smiled and watched, wondering if he might find an opportunity to join discreetly with the pack, blend with its eagerness to taunt some common foe, and escape. The leader gestured with the barrel of the pistol. Kagan pretended not to see. The soldier moved closer, trying to catch Kagan's avoiding eyes, then swung the pistol in an arc against Kagan's body. The blow bit clear pain through the skin and deep into the fibres of bone; a touch of quick, savage agony clawing at the senses, and an obscene image of missionaries passed through Kagan's mind. The soldiers were confused by his refusal to look at them, to play the part he ought to have known to play. But any plea now was the surest way to death. Another blow fell on the still convulting pain, and the agony shook in waves through his body. The soldier grunted and stood defiant, aware of his power, and tilted his head in show, and struck again. From the agony came hate, and an unbreakable determination never to acknowledge these curs' power over him. Somehow, some way, he would leave a wound in them and leave it to fester with memory. They screamed in rage at him, and pushed him with contempt from one to the other. For a moment they tired, then stepped back, and Kagan knew they were going to fire. He turned his back on them and watched the sky, the fear suppressing all thoughts as he waited for death.

He tensed and resisted the prod when the Indian officer touched him. The sense of life refused to come back, then came back with an awakened sense of the world, and of his inconsequence in it, and of each life's inconsequence to the universe.

The officer walked him as far as the door of the Palenbang, saluted, then walked away. Another war was over, a collection of days gone and now dependent on memory for their life, bringing no more to the faculty of mind than already existed in the received nature of ignorance.

Inside the hotel the missionaries, no longer swinging from list to list, linked arms and chorused good cheer in a jovial group. Kagan went upstairs and showered, and daubed iodine over the cuts and bruises. The old songs were being sung, meeting again over the grave of a war, as if it were the end of a year, as Kagan gathered his few remaining clothes and sat listening by the window, and waited again for others to move the world. There was no choice but to hang on, hang on as best he could.

The Red Cross truck brought them to the airport and the Canadian airforce transport rumbled heavily down the runway, lifted, and climbed slowly into the air. Very soon the land disappeared and the giant aircraft seemed to hum in space while the distant world moved under it. A smiling, happy, bosomly pleasant nurse gave Kagan his medical check-up, and tilted her head in mock bewilderment as she pushed back his shirt.

'Hey!' she laughed. 'You've been fighting.'

He shook his head. 'I'm more worried about the shirt.'

'Very brave. Haven't you another?'

'No.'

She went on testing, her smiles a little limited and unsure.

'Perhaps you'd like a disposable T-shirt?' she asked, finishing, 'It'll last 'til you get home, at least.'

He took it, walked down to the other end of the aircraft and into the shower-room, washed his last remaining shirt and left it draped over the rail to dry. Then he went back to his seat, settled in, and went to sleep.

At Brussels airport the Red Cross gave him a train ticket to Antwerp and a pass for one night's lodgings with breakfast in the Seamen's House. A note from the shipping company cried-off his contract. He had never set foot on their vessel and acts of God, war, and natural calamities on his way to it were not their responsibility. It was untrue, but it would take effort, time and money, to prove it. And Kagan was penniless.

The train arrived in Antwerp just before midnight. A cascade of Christmas lights glowed down the central streets and mellowed the fall of snow lying untouched and pure on the roofs. The passers-by strolled gently and unhurried, each on his own carousel, safe and secure in the warmth of their clothes and the prosperity and security of their lives. And Kagan's pass for a night's lodgings was too valuable to be wasted on a few hours' sleep. Five hours could be easily walked away, leaving him well placed to find a job on the spot market. Before five o'clock he could expect the agents to show on the fringes on the railway station and commence recruiting unregistered labour. But this was Antwerp, a city held autonomously by military deserters for a period during the last European war. And a city very conscious of its image as quartermaster for distant wars. Here, all the webbings of war were for sale, in strict respectability, but foreign males sleeping rough in railway stations or parks, or in any other haunts, ended their sojourns under the hose in a police carpark, and a shivering ride to the autobahn. That was the least, and the most merciful, treatment. So Kagan moved cautiously through the night.

At five he returned to the station. It was quiet and almost deserted. Some kindred spirits prowled about, as nervously and alert as cats. Others stood firmly in the middle of the concourse and gazed intently at the arrival and departure boards. But not a single agent was in sight. Kagan watched the kindred spirits. No one was smoking, no one checked the time on a wristwatch, no one wandered off for a coffee, no one had a newspaper. And at six o'clock, Kagan, almost the last to go, wandered away. A passer-by gave him directions to the Seamen's House, and there he learned the location of the Seamen's labour office. Tired groups of men lounged about the doors and along the street. Far too many to be taken up in one day's slack, even at the best of times. He went back to the Seamen's house and questioned the clerk. The labour office for shoreside work would not accept registration without a resident's visa; and a resident's visa could not be obtained from the police without proof of permanent accommodation. That involved a note from a resident accepting responsibility for his accommodation, or a receipt for rent paid for at least fifteen days in any establishment. And proof of sufficient funds for maintenance during that period. In this way the foreign labour was channelled into the unregistered labour pool, from where it could be deported. The clerk smiled. But the real catch was that landlords wouldn't rent accommodation unless you had proof of employment, and then you needed a month's deposit plus the rent. Again, the clerk smiled, and Kagan turned away.

At twelve o'clock he handed in his pass and received a roomkey. He went back onto the street and hustled a half-share for the best he could get: a third of the room's price. Other keyholders were hustling quarter-shares, and others were sub-letting as a business; selling thirds for something above a third-price, and clearing a profit. To stop it all the House would have to carry out hourly raids, or close down. So the smaller fish, at the lowest depths, and schooled to no other way, ate each other. Kagan let his companion into the room, then went out to buy food. When he came back he found the man huddled fully clothed in the bed, shivering and sleeping. Kagan took the chair to the curtained window, tossed the curtains over his head and over the back of the chair, and settled down to eat his groceries. On the sill some previous occupant of the room had neatly carved a quotation from something.

It read: 'Do to the book, quench the candle, ring the bell.' Kagan smiled, ate his bread and cheese, then laid his head on his folded arms and tried to sleep. Some hours later his companion awoke, and they sleepily and silently exchanged places.

The next morning he waited from four-thirty to seven in the station, the first to arrive and the last to leave, but still no job. Back at the House he ate the free breakfast, lay in the bed until eleven o'clock when all the rooms were turned out, then went out onto the streets.

Above all he needed a place to sleep. The days, even hungry days, could be walked away. But at night he needed a place to rest, to rest for its own sake, without fear of a cold water hosing and police hands.

There was no home to appeal to, a result of forgotten years of spite and resentment until spite and resentment faded with the memories, and the area of home grew more distant in his mind, became a contrived place of antiquated manners safe only in its insularity, a place to which he had to give sober and intent consideration, before he was re-convinced that it existed. It was a dream now, difficult to recapture, but leaving a mark on the senses, a mark of dulled distaste.

Those who had become friends with him over the years were kindred spirits of similar backgrounds, and similar predicament. He could no more find them now, than they could have found him.

The afternoon passed. Kagan noticed the trudge that had come over his walk. He returned to the Seamen's House to use the toilet. In despair he rested his head in his arms as he sat; and fell asleep. He spent the night huddled there.

The next day brought no respite. No work offered, and hunger began to burn and sear away the alert sense of embarrassment and shame he felt for his condition. It seemed that all his life he had been in the wrong; miscalculating, misjudging, mis-stepping, and all that he abhorred was right. Bowed and dull heads, and steady, regular plodding, led to snug homes, respectability, and pleasant, adjectivial lives qualifying as consequence. And there seemed no way of having the trappings of that life without the bondage, no way that common work, ungoverned by accumulation, brought security.

One more day passed, colder than ever, and every muscle and nerve in Kagan's body seemed to tighten into steel. One more night fretting in the cold of the toilet, until sickness came, and he vomited slow driblets of mucus and phlegm. His breath thickened with the smell of his stomach, coiled, and hung in the air about him. He left the cubicle and went back onto the streets, walking slowly, trying to will the lightheadedness away and re-focus his eyes. Then the ground dipped, and he skewed broadside across the pavement, forcing a startled pedestrian to skip and dart past. He steadied himself, and walked slowly and carefully on.

In the station an agent walked impatiently up and down and Kagan laughed, relieved of an invisible burden and feeling drunk and immaculately carefree, almost intimate and readily willing to comply with the agent's terms. Fast and brisk the agent stated the work, the pay, the shift, and Kagan nodded eagerly to each condition, wondering all the time at his own behaviour. He waited with the small group the agent had collected and tried to dispel the vagueness, the almost giddy vagueness that fanned across his mind. A hurt-looking, wizened man moaned about the twelve hour shift and grumbled unafraid; and Kagan, frightened, moved away from him. This day had to be fought and won in a lone battle; a livelihood, and a life, had to be restored, and defended. This was a war as deadly as any other, with its own deceits and its own barbarities.

He sweated mindlessly at the work for the first hour, crawling on hands and knees through a ship's bilges, digging the crusted muck, trying to breathe, pounding on the hardened slag and scooping it steadily into the slop buckets, bucket after bucket in the too-small space till he longed to tear at the metal with his fingers and punish it. The confined noise of the picks and hammers shook and trembled continually in the great hollow of the ship sitting between the cliff walls of the drydock. With no watch, with only cleared inch after inch to mark the time he cursed and fought and beat, raging, his overalls stuck like a leech to his skin with sweat and muck. It would never, never end. Time had stopped. But the fretting anguish and panic ebbed; and he calmed. Dry, grating pains ran through his chest and throat and he hammered inch after inch of the filth away. At each pause the muscles in his neck seized, bound, cramped, then unleashed themselves in packs of quivers and shook his whole body. He felt himself trembling, and easing, and worked on with a forming, cold hatred for the work, for himself, for what had made him; and he let the hate wash back and forth across his mind, enjoying it, smiling for its company, for the cool, calculating strength and rhythm of its power. And then he rebelled in the black hell of hunger and work. Like toys from childhood, every trait or habit he had ever known washed from his mind, every belief and conception lost its support, and his mind struggled clear and back to consciousness as a bright, newmade independence.

The amalgam of others, all that he had ever been, was defeated.

More than a day had been won. The umbilical cords, the mental puppet's strings that had made his life a fiction of himself, were gone. He thought of the young Englishman, and other men he had admired, and saw the check and catch that danced them to their personalities. And their unquiet, wondering consciousness of it.

The work finished. He peeled off the overalls and stepped under the shower in the changingroom. Some good-natured conversation broke out among the group as they tried to dry themselves with the paper towels. Then the hiring-agent stepped in, paid each the same cash sum of almost two days' pay, and slipped out again.

At the first store on the road back to town Kagan bought a bag of groceries and walked on, eating the raw slices of bread and sipping the milk. It was dark, and the soft snow lay gently on the street. He passed-by some railings and entered a small, circular park. A red painted sign with the famous legend 'Defense d'uriner' shined against the snow. Kagan ate more bread and milk and waited for his stomach to squelch and jerk and spew the sickly mess out onto the pathway. He watched the mess splash against his shoes. Never again. The blood of their war on these hands, but never again. The lives of farthing balls never again to rob his life of friends, and snugly plod on; and never again to leave him excommunicated from life, and deny him its bell, book and candle of existence. Even a routed army has leaders, and sends back scouts to torment the enemy. And sometimes the enemy claws at himself, in rage, and an animal of rebellion is born.

He walked on, out of the park and towards the Christmas lights, his name on no list to register his right to succour.

Brigitte

WHEN SHE OVERHEARD HIS NAME she had to see him. Jazz Murphy, unknown before, now grew in her childhood mind with the whispers and silences of the villagers. Jazz Murphy, only noted by the villagers as an idle curiosity, moved an affinity in her mind and promised relief from pressures she had never felt; until she overheard his name: Jazz Murphy.

In the classroom in the village school the commonplace, repetitious violence continued its daily, and now perceived, humiliation. To defy it and mock it, and not to learn, became a challenge that would absolve her of humiliation, and make her proud. And she could walk alongside Jazz Murphy, watch the earth pass under her steps, and wait for the acknowledgement that must come.

He walked her to the grounds of the summerhouse he had rented, rented because the Summer had gone and the house stood idle, and cheap to rent.

He took his haversack of groceries into the house and left her standing, outside, all her bravery in missing school just to walk with him, unacknowledged. But the affinity was worth it. When she saw him in the village she knew he was Jazz Murphy, knew it by the feeling that formed in her. It was natural to fall into step beside him, and feel the bond with another world, a world she might reach someday, and leave the childhood world where the most innocent step might lead into a universal abyss of disapproval.

He came back outside with a small, canvas-covered frame, some tins, a tray, and some brushes. Then he squatted on the ground and painted her likeness. She was embarrassed and pleased as her image emerged from the blots and strokes of paint on the canvas. She never knew she looked so free.

'What's your name?' he asked.

'Brigitte.'

And at the bottom of the painting he wrote: 'to Brigitte and that other world'.

Her first, unformed question was answered. He knew, and she smiled, smiled for having glimpsed the vague outlines of the frontier she was soon to cross.

*

The map on the wall showed the area of central London where Brigitte now lived, in a room of death-brown drabness. She turned in the bed, and placidly endured the drumming of the clock on the bedside chair. Then turned away again, coming in and out of the past, wondering if she would masturbate if she had never seen a man. And probably so. And where, then, was the sex in the attraction that had drawn her so surely to Jazz Murphy, six, seven, eight years ago today, when she was fourteen. If it had ever been possible to sublimate the drive it was sublimated then, and worked without her knowledge.

From the other side of the wall in this house, a house as partitioned into stunting, uninhabitable spaces as the Irish farms of her forefathers, she heard a body move and groan. She turned away, drifting back into sleep, and smiling as she watched the alarm clock jump in its mechanical excitement on the bedside chair.

*

Each day at noon the class rose for prayers to God. Afterwards, in covens of jubilation, they shouted again and again the well-learnt litanies of their catechism. It was a time of longed for joy, a time of remission, almost, from the pain that was used by the teachers, in all manners of casualness and deliberation, as an instrument of learning. After the long, humiliating morning the hunger for affection was warmly fed in the mystery of their God, and for whose glory they had been born. It took spirit, in the dark world of childhood, to defy both for the ease of sitting near a man she could not describe; only feel, in his presence, a world she had to find, and join her own vitality to its, and fuse into life. Only a child's spirit with its faith in a force of life complementary to its own, could endure the day-long silences of Jazz Murphy. And on the evening of the second day of her truancy from school, he gave her a picture of the thoughts she could not express. He signed it Ilya Ehrenburg, and the golden words on the canvas said: 'Read about us and marvel! — You did not live in our time, — be sorry!'

The praying to God ceased. 'Children,' the teacher said, 'Children'. And waited for the outward silences of the children to congeal.

'Children, the final disobedience in school is truancy. Truancy is a deceit, a lie. It is a sin. Sin humiliates our Lord Jesus.' She bowed her head and paused, then raised her head again. The superannuated language continued its slow passage and driving, inexorably, through the senses of the children, left them spiritless, mute, and submissive.

Brigitte's mind held the golden words of the canvas. She knew the key to the grammar of the other world's language, where she was strange, but not a stranger. She could endure the teacher's homily of excuse, endure the caning for truancy, endure it as she had to endure the darkness of childhood, with forebearance and a sigh, and her secret of Jazz Murphy. Brigitte smiled. Pride, the teacher said; one more sin. A deadly sin.

But the level of endurance had been set, and now threatened to be swamped as the teacher raised the lid of the desk and withdrew the leather strap. And with the bittermost pain to the edge of sanity the punishment was borne. When her eyes looked into the teacher's eyes they did not smile but gazed, without resolution. The scream came from behind, a high-pitched, hysterical —O, startling Brigitte back to consciousness of this world. She turned and saw the child standing, its arms hanging uselessly down, its twisted abject face, and the spreading pool of urine on the floorboards of the schoolroom. Brigitte walked away, an emigrant crossing an unknown frontier, and quietly walked the roads back to Jazz Murphy.

When she arrived her hardened hands, and then her legs, broke from their tension and trembled. It caused Jazz Murphy to coax, and talk to her, and share with her more of the world he knew, but he failed to alter the fixity of her eyes. Later he walked with her into the nervous austerity of her home, her father's wrath deflected by the unexpected presence and jovial expansiveness of the parish priest, and Brigitte's mother hovering expectantly over her arrival and the dining table posted with cake and biscuit.

The unsocial subject was dead, and this was its wake.

*

Brigitte woke again. She pulled the streetcoat up from the top of the bed and twisted into it, then slid her legs out and slipped on her flat-heeled, regular shoes. Then she shuffled, attractively, down the short, narrow room, out the door, and across the landing to the communal toilet. Artisan poverty was familiar to her, now, as familiar as it was to everyone else. But the ghost in her mind could make time run backwards, catch a segment of the past, and resurrect it breathing into the living present. A chilling tear of water from the age-crusted cistern overhead fell onto the small of her back, and carefully she lowered the tucked-up bottom of her coat further around her.

She moved back into the room, tightening the coat for warmth. Then she sat, and smoked, and watched the window, and waited in the cold for the kettle to boil and the electric fire to heat the room. This was the price, not of freedom, but of the flight from tyranny, and freedom stayed forever at the end of yet another road.

The kettle began to steam and Brigitte washed herself and combed out her hair. She dressed, prepared the tea, then knelt slowly, joyously, by her suitcase. She opened it, gently moved aside some clothing, unfolded a small towel, and beheld the glittering array of capsules. Her eyes closed, her tongue protruded, reverently, hesitant and anxious, almost trembled and held itself, almost unmoving, without ever touching her lips. She closed her eyes, received the two capsules, reached out piously for the tea, held its warmth between her hands, and tenderly sipped its sweetness. She breathed deeply, with softness and silence, then raised herself. She switched on the radio, listened to the music entering her brain, smiled in maternal joy, and sat back in repose on the chair.

The ghost was pacified. The music rippled higher and sweeter, became celestial, touched, then faded, indifferently, away. A female voice began its interpretation of the news as it spoke: an airliner had been hijacked. Brigitte laughed, alone, and switched off the insanity of a distant planet. Then she rose from the chair; and twirled as she put on her coat, and in her mind she sang for herself: 'Her eyes – they shone – like diamonds –'.

*

Two years had passed in another world. Jazz Murphy stayed and Brigitte learned to draw, to sketch, to paint, and learned, also, the joy of entering her mind and leaving the world behind. A protective cloak of strangeness covered her abasement in the daily school, the meals at home, the services of worship in the church, the common intercourse of banalities to acknowledge presence. Dependent for everything but her mind and the air, she lived on, clinging to her mind, built a world within, and nourished and sheltered it on dreams alone.

When the velvet longing touched her body hard, and demanded, and gripped, and shook away all other thoughts, and demanded, again and again, its presence to be acknowledged, she ran again, to fantasy.

In the paintings Jazz Murphy saw the force emerge, its innocent urge hidden in guilt and shame, and as smileless as Brigitte's bewilderment, while it groped its way towards cover.

And Brigitte didn't know how to speak of this, and mumbled, looked at the sky, smiled, and tried to skip girlishly, was awkward, and blushed. This was not to be spoken of. She went to church and prayed for forgiveness. For the aching for arms and legs and mouths and bellies, for the touch that would dispel the protesting wrath of denial, for the embrace that would hold her, and hold; then release her from its power.

Soon, against her will, it forced itself upon her, and soon its demands were accepted as another dark, childhood mystery. The other young women linked arms, laughed, hugged one another, playfully pushed each other away, pitched their voices hysterically high, and giggled, uncontrollably, joyously, on their way to bow their heads, suddenly humbled, and pray in the semi-darkness of the church.

Yet it hungered on, and made puppets of their wills. No one spoke of it, while it gave power to ambition and dreams, formed ambitions and formed dreams, and made of one and all secret confederates. But the traitor, fantasy, played one and all roles, bored of them, and lay back, sated; and contemplative. Then it looked about, and found its own neutral source, still undirected, unmarked, still unacknowledged. And always it was like this when it was sated, a force that would grow again to no purpose. And again and again, until its random stewardship was accepted, or periodically surrendered to in despair. There was no way to divert it, guide it, or husband it. Its winding desire was there to be suffered, a burden that would divest its energies, unchanged in their nature, to any activity. Then it became comically obscene, and contaminated those activities. And then it was no longer comical. That was all Brigitte could learn by herself.

Slowly, with guile and half-smiling shyness, she wandered back to the company of Jazz Murphy, to hours and hours of talk, accidental lilts in the conversations, to knowing eye catching knowing eye, and Brigitte burying her laughing face in her hands, glancing up at the one who seemed to have learned to co-exist tamely, unconcernedly, with the unreasoning force, and let it play, as a headstrong, boisterous animal, in the area of his life he ceded to it. But no more than that. No blind ambition, no lusts diverted to force other activities into the common shows of spurious adulthood. There was no need to sublimate the urge of curiosity, the urge to discover, to read, the urge to be happy. It was also impossible. Yet the silent confederacy upheld the heresy against the urge of sex, and made it as transparently hypocritical as the instruction of their young by the brain-washing terrors of beatings, and threats of beatings, in the dark, escapeless world of childhood.

Brigitte looked back from her other world, and saw the world that had held her for sixteen years as a cruel and merciless place. She knew her reaction was usual and common, reassuringly usual and common, but she knew she could not face that world as an adult. She retreated, nervously, from it, and into her world of talk, and books and books, the pleasure of finding herself comfortable there, and the world-relieving, speechless joy of paint and canvas creating reflections of her struggling mind.

When it was finished she closed her eyes in peace and rested for a moment, then looked once more at the strange and serene happiness of that plain, ungainly, and lovely girl painted faithfully on canvas. The unknown face of art, wearing its famous whispering smile.

Jazz Murphy came to look. 'A deVolterra came afterwards, and painted on the clothes.'

'The Mona Lisa was nude!' Brigitte was delighted. She looked again at the photograph, again at her painting. 'Vanity?' she asked, 'She thought Da Vinci wanted her?'

'It's a joke, Brigitte. A joke.' He cuffed her hair and wandered back across the garden and into the house. Brigitte gazed at the painting, tried to visualize the nudeness of the body to match the face. She looked at the face again. Slowly, she painted out the clothes, painted in the nude body. It was unsure, nervous, unsteady, but a revelation to Brigitte of nameless things. It puzzled her. Her world took on a more defined context, and the daily world moved further away into a sharper, more acute contrast. An exuberance of distracting things was needed before her mind, in solitude, assimilated the nameless feelings, grew to familiarity with them, and re-formed again to fluency.

Jazz Murphy was still inside the house. Brigitte walked to the door, paused, then called hello. She had never been inside the house, knew it was a refuge, a lair, that she must not disturb. He called to her to come in, and she entered cautiously, exploring the strangeness of the house and its atmosphere, and still uneasily aware of the sudden obscurity in her mind.

Jazz Murphy was sitting by the side of the fire, and Brigitte, with a silent diffidence, sat opposite to him. She watched the fire, but never looked when Jazz Murphy raised the tumbler of whiskey to his lips. She rose, went to the table, brought back the bottle of whiskey and refilled his glass. She left the bottle beside his chair, sat down again, and gazed into the fire. Her conscious mind was empty, yet the fixity of her eyes never altered.

'Brown study,' Jazz Murphy murmured.

Brigitte sighed, and continued to look into the fire.

'I never knew what happened that day,' she said. 'After you left, the priest and my father went outside and talked for hours. My mother sat beside me and put her arm around me, but never spoke. The rest of the family played about, quietly, as if a relative had died, a distant relative, and their mourning was unreal. So they neither really played nor mourned, properly. When I went to bed I could hear them talking. But not what they said. They were huddled in a group, whispering. When my sister came into the bedroom she didn't put on the light, and she lay as far from me as she could when she got into the bed. She lay as straight and still as a corpse, as if I might react to any movement and go mad. I didn't care. I'd always felt strange, everywhere. In the house, the school, in the village. But only strange, as if I had always half-forgotten them, but always knew them again. I'd never felt myself a stranger, an alien, before. Not to them. I'd never felt that beautiful detachment before, and so much peace. They were no longer real to me; the family, the school, the village. I became so happy, so happy. And there was you, and the feeling of homeliness I felt with you, and the life you came from.'

'They have always loved you, Brigitte. They sheltered you and fed you, and still love you.'

'I know. When I had to go back the next morning my mother brought me to the schoolgates, and gossiped with the teacher about food prices and the weather until the bell went. The teacher took my hand and walked in with me. "What a little darling you are, Brigitte," she said, "Sure you know I don't like to slap you. It hurts me more than it does you." Then I realised she was just an ignorant old cow.'

Brigitte rose and left the house, leaving Jazz Murphy smiling. And happy that two years before he had decided to remain with the kindred spirit of Brigitte, suffer the expense of renting permanent accommodation, and delight and rejuvenate his thirty-five years of living by answering Brigitte's basic questions about the impossibility of background and foreground both in focus, the confidence tricks our thoughtless eyes play on our minds. And her wondering, slowly phrased questions asking why nudes on canvas were conventional, nudes in photographs adolescent pornography, and nudity in public life forbidden. It made him re-examine assumptions that had unconsciously become convictions, and it was joyous to see again the world through the eyes of a child. When she tentatively introduced, with innocence and thoughtful pauses for delicate words, the possibility that she might pose for him, he dismissed the question before it was fully committed, changed the subject as if he had not understood properly, and directed her mind to other thoughts.

Earning a living to sustain his existence was not difficult. Uniform rows of plain, clean housing were rapidly expanding the suburbs of the Irish cities, and each house, almost, accepted the need of a picture over the fireplace in its sitting room. But pictures of studied mediocrity; pictures of the quietly murderous scenes of domestic bliss, pictures that aroused and affirmed the wonder of banality, the dream of instant, unshakeable social rank. The buyers looked and reacted, reacted with thoughtless eyes and cramped conventionality. And Jazz Murphy purveyed, in diluted greens and yellows, the supply of unperceived trickery and cartoons demanded by the social aspirations of the buyer. Yet it fed and housed him, and looking at Brigitte's empty place by the fire, he realised that a sixteen year old girl had taught him one more lesson.

The hopes that had fed his hunger from Greenwich Village to Venice, from Paris to Berlin, from early youth to the prime of adulthood, the hopes that finally brought him back to Ireland in search of a milieu that would nourish, and help him express, the forces of creation that worked within him, these hopes now became the hope of past dreams. When they returned now, they came in the moments between drunkenness and sleep, and robbed the drunkenness of its despair, gave purpose to his need for sleep. Brigitte's outburst of talk, and the reflections it caused in him, awakened those dreams again in his drunkenness. Tomorrow, tomorrow, he would work to the unfettered, uncompromised urgings of his dreams. And paint.

He took the bottle back to the table, rested and swayed against its edge, cursed himself a little, then stumbled into the next room and lay down asleep on the bed.

*

Brigitte walked through the settled gloom along the corridors of the bedsitter house. Outside, the London street was a row of uncared for, sad buildings boxed into warrens of bedsitters. Even a wisp of sunlight dappled a shade of respite against these grey, mournful facades. Brigitte never noticed; she had been immured to their atmosphere after six years of living in their midst. It was home to her now, with all of the little comforts and joys of familiarity. And often these comforts and joys, set against the bleakness of her crushed spirit, brought her great, unwarranted happiness, and whisperings of hope. She loved London, loved it for the refuge it had indifferently given her, for the abundance of its libraries, for the sheer freedom of its streets, and for the presence of the art galleries she never attended.

Imitation bohemians, and tourists, straggled past Brigitte on the street as she walked into Queensway, the fringe of downtown London. She read the newsvendors' placards. The hijacking of the aircraft was already in the evening paper. So too was the news that the eightieth terrorist bomb had exploded on the vulnerable pavements of this huge city. For the honour of an exclusive cause, the explosions smacked against the giant capital, shook fear into the inhabitants with all the force of wood slapping against flesh, leather slapping against skin, and engendered only rage and disgust, and contempt for the compliance they sought to promote.

She paused by the plate glass display window of a car showroom, cupped her hands and lit a cigarette. She sucked on the smoke, caught and swallowed it, and exhaled the burned odour of ganja. This was the last silent communion before the dullness of work. She stood and watched the luxury of the polished cars, the decorative price plaques that registered endless years of work. And she moved her eyes to watch her own reflection in the glass. Her eyes told her, awash in the sun of melancholy. The source and origin of trouble held no key to its solution. Broken bones are not healed by an analysis of the accident, and though it may prevent a repetition, it also resurrects the ghost of the pain. Brigitte's eyes knew this world held no cure for her; the accident was still in progress while she watched it happen, as she had before, without resolution. The sickness had to run its course, and the course led to the grave. She walked on, to Ercoles Photographic Studios, her workplace.

*

An hour after staggering drunkenly to bed Jazz Murphy awoke. Outside, Brigitte's easel still stood with the adulterated Mona Lisa pegged to its frame. An uneasiness settled over him and he moved quietly, strangely, in the darkened house. Nothing moved outside, but the foreboding remained, despite the unaltering stillness of the night. Consciousness of an undefined presence overtook him, and he patiently held his nerve, listening to the creaks and stresses of the house in the winter's night. Quietly, to aid the watch, he poured a measure of whiskey into a tumbler, and a noise, the same alien noise that had awoken him, sounded again against the normal noises of the night. Jazz Murphy relaxed, relaxed so that he could better maintain the vigil. Only hard, weather-beaten farmers could endure long in the night outside. And presently he heard the lurch of the easel being tugged from the ground. Then a silence that lasted, and the slow removal of the sense of dread that had penetrated his drunken sleep. He settled into the chair, drank some more whiskey, smoked, drank some more, went into endless repetitions of smoking and drinking, and finally slipped into a trance of peaceful sleep.

When he awoke it was past noon. Brigitte dallied by the door of the room with a nervous alertness of calm, self-consciously ready to spring anyway according to his mood. He sighed, embarrassed for the way she had found him, and for her reciprocated predicament.

'I'm sorry I blabbed so much last night,' she said, concerned with other things. 'I found this outside.' She handed him the phial of water. 'It's what they call Lourdes water, or holy water. They say it brings grace and banishes evil spirits.'

'Thank God,' he said, and drank it.

She smiled then, suddenly elated by his misunderstanding, and womanly indulgent towards the oddity of his innocence. It exalted her, and Brigitte accepted the change in their relationship without recognising it. Still smiling, and in an abundance of relief, she walked past him into the kitchen.

'Did they break the easel?' he asked, aware that they were other now than man and child in confederacy. He heard her laughter, free and blossoming, coming from the kitchen.

'I heard them whispering this morning. He turned the picture to the ground and,' Again her laugh blossomed, 'And made the sign of a cross over it with the water.'

'Your father?'

'Yes. Who else did you think.'

Jazz Murphy disliked the growing domesticity of her manner. This was not how he wished to start his day, any day. The memory of the drunken promise to himself in the moments before oblivion was still strong. To paint, in accordance with the force of creation; and restrained only by the truth of his ability. The pretentiousness of the wish troubled him in the sober daylight, yet there would be no choice now. The alert but casual surveillance by the villagers had been known to him, but he had never expected it to be fanatical. He knew of the webs of influence, carried by families and friends, that spun out of the meanest villages in the small island and into the heart of the cities, and into their institutions. Any scandal, differentiated from the normal by its non-conventional shades, would cause the web of relatives and friends to strive as mightily as a net against him. He might squirm and wriggle, and make out, but not for long. Outlets for his work were few, and their proprietors not people too fine of intelligence. They were discreet, and aware of their own vulnerability. They would not ignore warnings of pollutors, the warnings that would discourage their clients. It was too, too stupid, in this small island, the webs of superstititons, ignorance, secrecy and deceit. But they held the island's tiny society together; that was their brutal strength, and nourishment. And no alternative networks existed. Always, and ever, in such societies, morality is not the means, but the end. The means are governed by expediency and Jazz Murphy would be judged by that doctrine.

He rose and walked weakly into the kitchen. On the table Brigitte had already set two places for breakfast and filled the coffee cups. He took a cup, ignored the saucer and spoon and the delicacy of the set place, and returned to the room. Only last night, with its penetrating sense of dread, had he become aware of the vigilante aspect of the villagers. They were men continually close to the expedient slaughterings of nature, to the casual carrying of a fowl from among the squeals of its kind, and the casual wringing of its neck; to the looping of a noose around the neck of a dog that had tasted sheep's blood and stringing it up to hang from a rafter in a barn; and the hobbling of a cow, before the sledgehammer blows beat into its brain, the stab and pull of the knife across its throat, and the bucket underneath to collect the blood they later ate as congealed pudding with the stripes of bacon procured from the slightest tip of a knife into a pig's throat and its slow, slow bleeding to death, for the sake of the meat's bloodless flavour. The judgement of these men could only be tempered by expediency. They were too close to nature, and too far from ideals, to accept any questioning or disturbance of the values that secured survival. It was these values that gave rapacious strength, and opportunism ever alert for any advantage, to the sons that migrated to the cities where the guise of affected civilities merely bemused their clear eyes ever set on survival; and their intimate knowledge of the merciless in nature. It promoted their savage pursuit of success even in the most gentle fields of endeavour.

Jazz Murphy wanted to paint one honest picture, one honest picture to strip away the filth of mediocrity his survival had accumulated. But no picture would paint those thoughts that now shadowed his mind; and left him unconscious of Brigitte's worried face as she silently watched his eyes struggle for a solution. He thought of the shooting stars that came and disappeared, of the black doors in space that devoured all but the door, and sent shooting stars into parallel universes. — O, the pictures he wanted to paint, of the corpses that compounded the planet, produced its grass and food, and fed the animals to procure the sperm and ovum that transubstantiated life and resurrected yet another consciousness. Flesh of our flesh, blood of our blood. I must die, therefore I am. The picture he might paint, and it might show, life forever coming from the primeval slime, our flesh and blood, in the endless space that warped time, leaving endless, arenaless space where speed could not exist without a measurable arena. What pretension of colours would convince the thoughtless eyes that humankind was not a vanity apart from the universe, with a destiny different to the universe.

Brigitte touched his hand, and held it. And Jazz Murphy reached and took her into his arms, wondering at the concept of a god's strange factory for the manufacture of souls.

'Paint, Brigitte. People and scenery are always there to see. But look into your mind. Analyse the inner force of the outward show. Paint that.'

She lay against him, happy and excited. She felt at one with the forces of creation that gave birth to meaning, at one with a comrade in that struggle. And words began to decline, then faded to uselessness as their minds moved to silent empathy and union through the senses of the body. They caressed and kissed and moved their hands over their bodies in their unseeing unity of mind striving with mind as the pliant power of their bodies shook and stormed and strained for the desire of endless unity, for the unity that would hold and release them into one. And for those moments eternity vanished, and quietly, gently, returned with their consciousness of this world. The ghost had slipped away and now returned as their high swells of breathing eased, and ebbed on the threshold of peace in each others arms.

They lay together, head side by side with head, in memory of the lifetime they had lived in a moment.

Brigitte moved, a sylph celebration of joy in each movement of each limb. Her features seemed smoothed, composed, and no whispering smile lingered in her eyes. She walked to the window and watched the sky for moments, then turned and smiled across the room at Jazz Murphy.

And when he made coffee for her she ignored the spoon and saucer, and maternally held the warmth of the cup between her hands.

The great, strong weariness of longing that had yearned and caressed her body in tightening folds of velvet, yearned in pain for the embrace of unrelenting love, had dissolved into freedom. For the first time in her life happiness had become a form of reality, reserved within herself, and nourishing flickering rays of strength and confidence against the menace of living outside her nature.

'I still go to confession, you know,' she said, and turned to look out the window.

'You've just been, Brigitte.'

The remark was smirkless, without malice. Jazz Murphy, twice as old, wondered what penance might be required of him; and wondered what more would follow. Brigitte's temperament, and her idyllic trance of contentment, would not escape the conclusions of the dour, canny villagers. Nor least of all her family.

'Don't worry,' she said, 'I can lie.'

'There's no point in that, Brigitte, if you accept their right to judge.'

She sighed, almost like a patient child, knowing Jazz Murphy did not comprehend the concept of God, and found it hard to accept the intelligence of those who did. And their worship, of all kinds, baffled him.

'When I first started to visit you, they asked me why you didn't attend church. I told them you were a christian, but didn't practice.

Do you know what that means to them?'

He shook his head.

'It's like the water; so long as it's been blessed it doesn't matter whether it works or not. It's the faith they can put in it that matters then. But it doesn't have to practise its value. It's blessed. That's enough. And you don't have to practise either. You're still one of the fold.'

'The fold.'

'Yes. The herd, the fold. Otherwise they wouldn't have trusted me with you. They believed you were no more a threat to my fingered virginity than anyone else.'

Silently, Jazz Murphy began to drink. After his lifetime of dodging herds and folds, of all kinds, of living in this no-man's-land between groups, of passing their emigration guards at the exits and the immigration guards at the entrances of each tribal frontier, he knew the force of their confident mob power, their inability to collectively reason, and their angry arousal at the slightest whiff of prey.

Brigitte spoke of leaving the village, then of staying, and defying the herd, the fold. They talked all day, and all day Jazz Murphy knew there were no options. Like lying to false gods, running turned defeat into a rout, staying meant turning the other cheek; and annihilation of themselves by the demands of its conventions. Each outward bow to the demands of village respectability would take on an inner form, and finally mould them to the outward show.

Night came, and they lay silently in each other's arms. The next night the villagers punished Jazz Murphy, and days later Brigitte arrived in London, her eyes staring without resolution on any object, but her hatred for the fold that had nursed, fed, and reared her; and would have been her lifelong, stable companions, had she broken to their will.

Jazz Murphy eased himself from pain into death. The planets continued their weary orbits, repeating the cycles that humankind numbered as years to facilitate its delusion of progress, while bombs smacked the city streets in punishment, humans killed each other for love of their exclusive herds, for the symbols of nationhood that curtailed to its borders its commitment to humanity, and reduced self-determination to the collective will of the mob. For this they unselfishly gave up their lives in sacrifice, out of love for their exclusive mob identity, its most sincere killers the most idealistic, as if the village, fold, herd, nation, took its life from a different source and held a destiny different to the rest of humankind. And Jazz Murphy, like all rebels and mutineers in the human army, was punished more for the example he set than for any hurt inflicted on the tribe. And later he eased himself from pain into death.

*

Brigitte's employer, Ercole, was long hardened to exile, and to the purposelessness it placed in the eyes of those who lived in its no-man's-land. It was an expression so unlike the clear-eyed, affirmed arrogance of those who identified with their herd's insular and exclusive traditions, used language as an expression of creed, and believed the words of its vocabulary essential to their identity, veritable definitions of their uniqueness in the world.

Ercole watched Brigitte as she entered, noticed the emptyness in her eyes, and returned to his work. Brigitte lit a plain cigarette and joined Ercole at the workbench. Each knew the job well, knew the other's ability, and worked together in silent harmony re-touching the photographs of wedding parties, family groups with the new baby, coming of age celebrations, and the exuberance of models in product advertisements. Their brushes gently moved, and dimmed the carnivorous brokenness of exposed teeth, slimmed a bride's leg, removed the unseeming blink of obscenity from a guest's unconscious leer, lessened the rigid awe in the children's faces, and tried hard to curtail the smirk of vanity that often betrayed the prematurity of the coming of age celebrations.

It was false and purposeless work, and they did it unthinkingly, their minds far away in peace and tranquility.

Of all of Brigitte's years in London this was the happiest, the one least marked by despair. From the first moment of her arrival in Euston Railway Station, stranded suddenly in the expanse of its concourse, alone and frightened without any way of knowing whether to go right or left or straight on, without having any place to go, and the massive immobility of strangeness surrounding her, immobilising her, leaving her staring intently and bewildered, as if she had arrived on another planet, this was the first year when panic had finally subsided, slipped beneath the passing years, and left her more resigned to disappointment.

There was nowhere to turn. The concourse emptied and filled with tides of people, people who knew where they were going, people to whom the London placenames held an abundance of information, and to whom London was not a place as incomprehensible as an unknown language. It roared into Brigitte's face and dismissed her as stupid when she could not understand the incessantly repeated information.

All that Brigitte had learned of survival she had learned on the run, learned by trying to assess situations rationally, only to find they unpredictably changed the moment she acted. From the moment she strolled deliberately coatless from her parents' home to contrive an opportunity to catch the village bus, lying to the familiar driver and seeing his disbelief, then lying with hints of sweetening promises that gave him an interest in confederacy, and silence, after the bus arrived at the first railway station; from deliberately walking away from the railway station to further deceive the driver, and her stealthy, fugitive return by backstreets to the empty station and its bored, suspicious clerk; and from there to the anonymity of a city she had chosen to deceive any pursuit, Brigitte's run was continuously faltered by the countless unexpected changes each new move brought. Without the loadstone of London forever guiding her she would have fallen, and the despair and rage that would have overtaken her then still frightened her.

In Dublin she bought an overcoat, clothes, and a suitcase. And a few hours later watched the evening cloudlets, burned at their edges and turned to orange by the setting sun, drift languidly across the peaceful sky. The ship cleared the narrow opening of the harbour, and Brigitte viewed the land of Ireland for the last time. Other passengers walked about the decks and Brigitte, too frightened and timid to spit, cursed the land under her breath.

Three hours later she landed, safely, in Great Britain. She passed the immigration guards at the port after endless questions about her identity, her lack of identity papers, her reasons for wanting to come to Great Britain, as if it were an emotion they did not easily understand. Then she answered questions about her finances, and was allowed to enter. But not before her belongings were searched by yet other guards.

All this was strange and surprising, and hostile, to Brigitte. It hurt her to be treated so in the land of her childhood's loves, the land of Dickens, Marian Evans, Austen, the Brontes, of Forster's civility, the land, even, of Shakespeare. Yet already it was so different, as if they had all omitted, never recognised, an essential dimension. Even when abroad, even outside the Empire, they had never known the feeling of foreignness, had never left the incubating warmth of their nationality, never suspected what they enjoyed so unthinkingly. Not even the singular Maugham. None had outgrown the acquired taste of their upbringing, the ethos of nationality.

And now, on the open concourse of Euston station, Brigitte felt herself an alien in a land she had thought would be more home than home ever was. It is always like this, that pecular taste of an exile's loneliness, even in her own country. It separates the exile from the immigrant. No longer a partisan of her origins and no wish to regress into a partisanship of identical childishness.

She had never anticipated what would happen immediately after her goal of arrival in London had been achieved. Just to arrive had been the strengthening urge. And now, on fulfilment, it evaporated.

Time was needed to assimilate and reconcile this reality. She bought an Irish newspaper and tried to enter the station restaurant to sit, and ostensibly read, and give her mind time to find a solution. A waitress, callous and powerful, screamed: 'No bleedin' suitcases.' and turned away. Brigitte heard but said, in shock, sorry. The waitress turned back, 'It's wrote there, isn' it.'

Brigitte left and searched the station for a luggage office. The porter was black. He listened to Brigitte's accent, noticed her disorientation and vulnerability, and smiled. And an echo of an idea came to Brigitte's mind in response to his kindness.

She walked back across the concourse that somehow seemed slippery and odd to walk on, and she missed the company of her suitcase. She smiled at the thought and entered the restaurant. Inside, the insipid tea, slopped onto the saucer in its delivery, was ignored after the first sip, and the sight of the teabag, in the curdling milk surfacing like a dead, bloated body. In the newspaper she read that men, in some stupid, exclusive street, had forced a man to lie on the ground, and then fired their pistols into the back of his knees. A shiver of anguish passed through Brigitte for the trembling pain of the man's agony.

Brigitte wanted only a room to live in, a job to support her and the insulation of her loneliness against the madness of the world. The knowledge that she was already defeated had not yet congealed in her mind.

She left the restaurant and returned to the luggage office. The porter, in between handing cases in and out, explained the roulette of finding a bedsitter, a place to live, in the capital city. She could search London for days or weeks and always find the rooms already let before she arrived, spend badly-needed money travelling to and from places that only the desperate could accept as human accommodation. The porter knew; he had walked the same treadmill on his innocent arrival in London so many years before. And nothing had changed. All he could do was to give Brigitte the address of a house near where he lived in Finsbury. And slowly and simply, understanding the dense foreignness of London through Brigitte's eyes, explained how to travel there.

Then Brigitte faced, for the first time in her life, the terror of the escalators that brought her down, and further down, into the rabbit-curved tunnels of the transport system. The handleless doors of the train opened and closed automatically. And in her fear, Brigitte understood why Londoners called these tombs and trains 'tubes'. From station to subterranean station the train started, jolted, accelerated, de-accelerated, stopped, jolted again, and then the doors slid open, as if the train were a worm feeding and excreting through its pores. People squeezed in and out of the packed compartments with casual, light, comfortable indifference. It seemed that the beliefs of zoomorphism, and the beliefs of reductionism, were no longer heresies in this underground world.

Just past the ticket-collector's barrier at Finsbury station, and in the blind defiant trance of shock, Brigitte pushed her suitcase against the wall, sat on it, and smoked cigarette after cigarette, and ignored as imbecillic the frowning stares of passers-by on their way to and from the looking-glass. Then she walked street after street, stopping again and again to ask direction, and walked on and on, the burden of the light suitcase growing with every step. When she reached the guest-house, all sense of direction, and of purpose, were lost.

She rented a room to share with three other women. They were at work, and Brigitte lay down in the privacy of the drab, dis-spiriting room and stared vacantly at the ceiling. This was the end of the journey, this emptiness its fulfilment. This was the place she would call her home; and its limp, implacable depression, without a murmur, singly smothered every hope.

The first of her room mates to arrive back from work was Irish; and from her Brigitte learned it was the nationality of everyone in the house. She had run in a circle, and the dull, heavy weariness of it all no longer mattered. All that remained was a deep anguish to be alone, to give in, to give up, to close her eyes and lose consciousness forever, only to be alone, to fix dead eyes on the past, undisturbed, and to grieve.

'Run away, have you?' asked the other girl.

'I'm only staying here a night,' Brigitte answered.

'Suit yourself,' said the girl, in no manner of offence, and curled herself up comfortably to read the tabloid evening paper.

Brigitte stayed three months. Her room mates were coarse and crude, in Brigitte's eyes, for their benighted unconsciousness of the trivialities they cheerfully accepted as the fulfilment of life. In either office or factory they worked cheerfully, and mindlessly delighted in conforming, chicly, to the taboos and niceties that permeated their set. Marriage and children might or might not come, but homely little comforts gave deep contentment, and life would be pleasantly whiled away with no seditious questions to excite and vex their minds. Their expectations were less and they enjoyed life more. And Brigitte felt disturbed by that, unable to see its lie. Yet on trivial things they passed their lives more happily than Brigitte and lived only for jokes and the camaraderie of workmates, the disco-dance rituals of mate selection, and the winking conceit of sexual awareness that they never troubled to understand. Other animals, lesser animals, shared the same playfulness and passions, and enjoyed them to a greater extent. Yet Brigitte's room mates lived peacefully, accepted sorrows and disappointments as seasons that would pass, munched their chocolate bars at night, and often laughed, unexpectedly.

When Brigitte tried to speak to them of serious things they became blank and distracted by inconsequential oddities, like children on a strange day in a village school, as if the plane of existence had tilted, and they were afraid of losing grip, and the realities collapsed into the black doors in their minds, never to be spoken of, and impossible to pursue. No ecstasy of oceanic beauty, craving for embodiment in life, this life, ever touched their consciousness. They shook their heads at such mysterious notions. As becoming as children, they smiled lovingly at Brigitte's mention of such things, then with fresh playfulness and zest, turned away to wonder and absorb themselves, in quiet delight and joyousness, with handfuls of sand.

Using another name, the name of another, older girl from the village, Brigitte applied for workpapers and found a job. The routine of work in the factory canteen helped stabilise her life and the unaccustomed severity of the job left her little time to brood between work and sleep. When she hardened to the work, and needed less and less sleep to recover, she spent the extra hours of freedom in the company of her room mates. And soon she cursed herself, blamed herself, for the discontent that shadowed her life, and made her impatient with the ignorance of her room mates, their antics, and the reptilian natures that gin brought to the surface, and for their unconscious, peristaltic courting of boys and men, so sexual in its display and so visually displeasing. And for the value they placed on their virginities, as if its riddance made them victims of a pagan sacrifice.

Brigitte grew more and more silent in their company. With her work and her companions she could not live in her time, nor could she learn to live in theirs. She searched, in nightly trudge after nightly trudge, for an affordable single room, and finally found one in an area of decaying slums off the Commercial Road in London's East End. She changed jobs, and moved away without goodbyes. And at the end of each day's work she returned to her solitary haven, happy and content once inside its door. Yet outside its security a growing nervousness attached itself to her. She believed she could sense people of her time, of her community of experience and aspiration, and with these she had an immediate and settled empathy. Those not of her time, neither inferior nor superior to her, but not of her time, frightened her with increasing ease, and without their knowledge, and became more and more incomprehensible as she feared their animal wrath that lurked, visible, in their confident poise and mannerisms, in the strength and certainty of their displayed beliefs. Brigitte feared violence, but more fearful was its perpetual threat, its growling promise of arrival from a source less reasonable than the flight of a bird, a source that could never be reached nor altered in any way. And the twist of the submissive dread of violence was her instinctive knowledge that to combat it effectively she would have to release, never to re-capture nor re-control, the same destructive source within herself. This was the source of dread. It would capture the brain, become its master, use that talent for its own ends. And she would become the type of person she feared most, was most nervous of, and most despised.

When anyone sensed her timid, hiding nervousness, sensed the fear that almost shook her body in its demand for control, they smiled at her, with either sympathy or contempt, but always with superiority. They had never fought this force, never recognised its command in their unearned peacefulness and calmness. And Brigitte had never been taught to expect this fight of adulthood, nor how to cope with it.

The lady caught Brigitte's eye; and she and Brigitte knew. The lady's walk across the canteen floor was not a stroll, nor in any way affected. It had the sway of unconscious grace. Brigitte followed and handed the lady a menu.

'It isn't quite good today, Miss,' she said in her normal subdued manner. The lady laughed, low and casual. 'Lord, child. I know.'

The neutral words rang, and for a gracious moment Brigitte felt a balm of peace. This woman had triumphed.

'I'll have a tea, thank you.'

Brigitte returned to the kitchen and passed on the order. She thought of the understanding in the voice, the ready skill of the words and their awareness of the other-worldness of the exchange. She brought the tea but the lady seemed indifferent to it.

'Why are you working in a canteen?' she asked quietly. But other people were in earshot and Brigitte glanced at them and back to the woman, but made no reply.

An hour later she came and took Brigitte aside in the canteen. 'I've made an appointment for you,' she said, 'Don't worry. She's an excellent doctor. But you must go tonight.' She handed Brigitte a paper with the name and address and appointment time: 6.30. Then she was gone and Brigitte never saw that lady again.

She cut work, went home for a change of clothing, went to the public baths, emerged clean and bright and hopeful, and arrived at the doctor's an hour too early. It was a childish, girlish thing to do. But in that same childish, girlish attitude was the understanding that she needed help, but didn't know, and wouldn't have known where to look for the kind of doctor she needed. And now she had learned both.

She gave her name at the door and the receptionist, without curiosity, quietly showed her in. With equal quietness a loudspeaker in the waiting room called out names at indeterminate intervals. Brigitte sat with an anxious alertness and rose immediately when her name was called. She went back to the foyer and the receptionist pointed out the consulting room. Brigitte turned, and stumbled in her step, glanced back quickly to see the receptionist smile in a comradely fashion and nod towards the door. Brigitte opened the door and entered the room. It was bare. No paintings, no decorations, no carpet. Just a desk and a chair on either side. Brigitte thought it was an ante room and stood, staring frozenly at the woman sitting behind the desk. For a moment too the doctor did not understand, then she motioned to Brigitte to close the door and indicated the chair opposite her.

The preliminaries were easy; the factual questions of age, family structure, previous medical history. And then the psychiatrist found herself against the wall of Brigitte's silence. To her best efforts she received nods and whispered answers of yes and no. And with these to guide her sketched the background of Brigitte's childhood and its environment. She saw the struggling wish in Brigitte's eyes to break the force that held her frightened and silent, to rationally and unemotionally answer, and explain the brute force within her that demanded her blind obedience to its will. The doctor's emotional detachment from the subject fascinated Brigitte, and now she listened as the woman indifferently explained the evolution of the conflict in the brain, the triune brain of humans that held, still, the ancestral brain common to reptiles and the ancestral brain common to mammals. These worked in harmony and co-ordination and gave humans instincts and feelings. Scientists called them the limbic brains. But they were not subdued nor properly co-ordinated to the brain of the neocortex that gave humans their intellectual capacity. And thus the frustrating conflict between rational thought and irrational behaviour. A well-balanced individual was one who balanced limbic and neocortex. It was a never ending, standoff fight.

Brigitte smiled. She had a ghost of an idea but couldn't catch it. 'Where does that leave me?' she whispered. But the doctor didn't smile. 'Why is your righthand more useful than your left?'

'I'm lefthanded, Doctor.'

'But you see the point?'

'I use it more, of course.'

'Because you have used it more. You were allowed to.'

And she returned the conversation to Brigitte's childhood. Back to the moment of birth, and the terror of entering the world of blinding lights, deafening noise, the terror of unknown hands, and the child's fanatical, animal determination to live, to cling to safety, and its endless, animal devotion, and animal suggestibility, to whatever shelters and feeds it. All as naturally as it suckles, as naturally as a serpent crawls away from its egg and a foal walks moments after birth. The limbic is highly developed at the birth of the body, and is strengthened and reinforced without delay. It must be. But the human brain receives no cooing and petting, and is left unfed.

'You were spoilt in childhood, Brigitte. You are loving and respectful, but it proceeds from animal cunning, not rational evaluation. You don't know why you are loving and respectful, or resentful and rebellious. What is certain is that you were taught to be whatever you are. The knowledge you learned of any subject, in or out of classrooms, was taught to facilitate the ability of the animal, not the intellect. Otherwise you would not be more or less badly balanced. You would have subdued the animal, and you would be immensely gifted. Acquiring knowledge is a function of memory, but its use is solely the function of intellect. That is why there are highly educated but stupid people, even psychiatrists.'

The doctor smiled, for the first time during the interview.

'I find it difficult to believe, doctor.'

'Yes.'

'I do want to be myself, not what I was moulded into.'

'For some reason your intellect wants total dominance. It doesn't in most people, the contentment of the limbic is more pleasing. But your intellect is undernourished and unexercised. Spoilt, I said. It is afraid of more punishments, more defeats of reason, it knows that unquestioning devotion to any cause, from politeness to religion, is more rewarding and peaceful than continual evaluation.'

A look of weariness and resignation came over the doctor's face. She looked at Brigitte for a moment, then reached for the prescription pad. 'Brigitte, your intellect may be spoilt beyond repair. And it is trying to take on a well nourished, unspoilt faculty that has the cunning of a snake and the willpower of a mule.' She smiled again. 'Your intellect associates learning with pain and humiliation. How can you hope to develop it?' Then she gave Brigitte the prescription and the first and last interview ended. This was a death sentence. Adult life had been defeated before childhood ended. Unbelieving as it seemed it accorded with Brigitte's condition, the village, and the girls of Finsbury.

Brigitte was a few months away from seventeen full years of life, and all she knew of the nature of her body, the nature of her brain, she had learned from self-examination, observations, novels, from a commonplace painter, and from a kindly psychiatrist who casually accepted that people did not want to know the source of their beliefs, their convictions, not even the source of their own, and acknowledged, occasional bouts of irrational behaviour.

The chemist queried the doctor's prescription, and Brigitte never took a script to a chemist again, preferring, forever, the dangerous anonymity of the street sellers. Without insight, without courtesy, he questioned her boldly in the public square of his shop. Brigitte stood, immobilised by panic, in the echoing silence of his unanswered questions. And repeatedly the word drugs kept punching out as an insult; the chemist's own cure for Brigittes' types. He knew the type, and with animal cunning and power he despised them. Then he 'phoned to the doctor to confirm the prescription. And in the interval Brigitte cringed under the eyes of the other shoppers; those buying face powders, scents, lip paint, eyelash colourers, and beauty masks. She did not live in their time, and that was her only consolation.

Desolate, depressed and stripped of public and self-respect, she returned to her home, the jar of capsules held tightly in her hand. When she closed the door of her room behind her, she breathed properly for the first time in hours, then lay, too damned to care, face downwards on the bed. For a little while she drifted into sleep, then awoke to the still, lonely silence of the sheltering room. She smoked for a while, made some tea, and fidgeted about the room. Then she took her first capsule: one hundred milligrams of largatyl.

In a little while her back began to hurt, and a pressure gently stretched itself along her spine. She stood and stretched her arms, the force pulling along her body, reached up, forced herself, and touched the ceiling with the tips of her fings, then rose higher and pressed her palms against the ceiling. The giant force still swept along her spine, rippled its fingers across the loosening nerves, slipped them free, and caressed the ecstatic waves of release that followed. Brigitte stripped, pulled back the bedcovers, and stretched her deliciously aching back against the cold sheet. The nerves tingled > *music* < in rainbow symphonies of colours moving through her. For endless minutes, for minutes that would never die in her mind, she lay in the glow of colours, awash in oceanic beauty and wonder, her mind and body a receptacle to the gentle awe of the universe. The smile on her face was a whispering enigma, a work of nature's art; and Brigitte moved her stretching and easing body to a cooler part of the sheet —O, but music, music. Music to sweeten the sweet music of the air.

She dressed herself without care and slipped happily down the stairs and into the street, its old decaying slums radiant and at peace in the universe. Near Limehouse she found a bar with a disco-lounge. She entered, asked no one, left them to their beauty, and danced with her freed body to the trembling pitch of the electric guitars. She was not alone, loveliness was palatable in every movement, in every sway of the body, every sound, in this mere glimpse of heaven.

A black girl approached, said 'Hi!' and danced with her. They smiled into each others smiles and moved their bodies. The delicious music screamed its bodyless joy of mind. 'How d'you feel, love,' the girl asked. 'Like the holy ghost,' Brigitte answered, 'Like the fucking holy ghost.' And they fell giggling into each others arms. 'Me too,' said the girl, 'Me too, sister.' And they danced on.

Finally, the music switched off. The bar was closing. Outside, Brigitte and her friend, Huldah, and some kindred spirits, gathered into a group and wandered down the East End streets. Not far away was the famous Sidney Street, now a neat row of Government built housing, for part of its length. Nearby, too, were the streets where the people of the East End had defeated the British Nazis in a pitched battle less than forty years before. A little further away was the now abandoned synagogue that had given the refuge of its sanctuary to those who refused even the non-combatant roles in the last major war of the European groups. And nearby, too, the house of the Jewish tailor who stitched the seditious message 'Workers unite' into the tunics he sewed for the army.

These streets had an honour no city in the world could match. And that night was beautiful in those streets. Brigitte's mind soared, and splashed free, from pain, humiliation, the constraints of primitives. Her mind rose to its time; time was grace and Brigitte its angel. It was a nice feeling, and she smiled to herself for its innocence.

The loudspeakers stood on upturned beercases in the corners of the basement. This was the Calendar Club, a club of makeshift refuge that frequently changed its location from one abandoned, blockaded house to yet another condemned house in the slums. But always it was the Calendar Club, despite police raids, and the grapevine always knew the new location.

Brigitte and Huldah danced in the soft smell of burnt ganja smoke. And Brigitte wondered what it was. But the universe was music, hugging, squeezing, moving the body to the freedom of the mind. Music, music, hug me, hug me, music hug me, love me. Music give sound to these vibrations, wash me clean, music lift me out of this dying body. Music, mother, music, hug me, let me go, hug me. MUSIC!

And together all were one. All danced as if free of their bodies, only the shadows on the broken walls told them they moved with animal forms, their elbows swaying wildly over their rolling hips, but their minds had escaped to freedom, to an eternity of joy. The music said it: Ground Control had lost Command.

Brigitte sat against the wall and started to laugh. Huldah danced on. Another girl sat down. 'What you on?' she asked, laughing. Brigitte laughed through her eyes. Tears ran down her happy face and she pulled her legs up to her chin. Her body shook, mirthful as a child's, and she rocked herself back and forth, fighting in joy with her laughter. Huldah handed her a beer and a handrolled cigarette, and sat next to her.

London; and Brigitte was almost seventeen years old, sitting in the basement of a derelict house, drugged, smoking ganja, feeling the balm on wounds hands could never reach, wanting no hands to ever again reach for her, to twist and mould her into their sick images of gods and right and wrong, but to let the music enter her head and unwind her body, to give to herself the peace to know herself, again, to love herself as a child watching the earth move under her steps, to forget forever the factory-training schools, to forget the factories, to forget the animal filth and grime unknown hands slapped into her life and made of her an animal also, frightened to blind obedience, afraid of the cold and emptiness of the world, afraid to catch at those hands with the force of death, catch those hands and tear them from their arms, and never be beaten again, never again satisfied with the closed door of a stunted, partitioned room, a book, and a bar of chocolate. And to touch once more the fabric of canvas, and feel herself flowing with the colours into the painting.

Then the spasm passed. The ganja tasted sour and Brigitte coughed, struggling to sip some beer and restore her breathing. She understood and asked Huldah the price, but the girl shook her head and smilingly handed her another. 'It's doing you no good,' she said, 'Why pay?'

A feeling, the slightest feeling, that she could move without motion, transfer herself to the other wall without moving her body, change it to move to her, passed through Brigitte's mind with a clear easy logic. She could transfer herself to the other wall without motion. Then she felt she had; and looked across at herself looking at herself. She knew it was wrong, but the easy logic said no, and she felt as if she had awoken looking into a mirror and had no feeling to tell her what was substance, which its reflection. And then the mirror moved, spiralled, and the images changed from place to place without motion.

'How d'you know it's doing no good?' she asked Huldah.

'Cos you ain't high, and you ain't been sick.'

But Brigitte felt that if she dreamed she could explain it. A dream about herself, and the dreamed-self felt she had substance also, but was merely Brigitte's sleeping mind dreaming, and only the merest part of the original mind, yet the dreamed-self had all the dreams and knowledge of the original mind. Nothing need ever really move.

Then the ganja caught, its nausea convulting Brigitte. She ran across the room and into the corridor, into a corner, and spewed a light sickly mess onto the floor. She wiped her mouth and wandered back into the room. Her head cleared. Unquestioning, serene peace breathed in and out of her mind. All was gentleness, but she was tired, and adrift in an unknown sea of calmness. She gave Huldah her address, asked her to visit, then wandered slowly around the quiet roads until she found a familiar landmark, then went peacefully home, weaving along the pavements with the innocent airs of childhood.

At home, in bed, she turned once in the blankets, the smooth comfort of her body caressing her serenity, and fell happily into a deep, untroubled sleep.

*

At home in the village in Ireland they heard that Brigitte was working in a factory canteen in London. Someone had recognised her. She appeared quiet and subdued and it seemed she had learned her lesson.

Jazz Murphy's landlord called a man of a religion to visit the house of the dead tenant. The man came, chanted some words from room to room with the solemnness, the sincerity, of the hypnotised, repeatedly kissed the crucifix he held in one hand, and sprinkled water about as he spoke.

Then the landlord found another tenant.

*

When Brigitte woke it was six o'clock. Six o'clock in the evening. It amused her. She lit a cigarette and got a buzz on the first drag. Life was beautiful. She hummed to herself, wished she had a radio, washed her face and hands, brushed out her hair, and dressed. She wondered if Huldah would come. When she said her name, and remembered their affinity of spirit, she remembered another who had entered her life, given it the flavour of another dimension when most she felt suffocating and cringingly conforming, until she saw the rescuer, and smiled, once more in safety.

Huldah arrived while Brigitte was still smoking her first plain cigarette. With her afro hair, her plain jeans and sweater, she looked happily composed, relaxed, and ready to enjoy the happiness the world had to offer. She'd spent the day sleeping, too, and Brigitte wondered, passively, how Huldah lived; where the money came from. But it was of no great importance.

They got off the bus before it arrived at Piccadilly, and went to eat at an American cafe. Brigitte ate with a glorious delight, and relished more and more of the food, but Huldah just picked indifferently. Then she put a hand on Brigitte's, winked, and slid out of the booth. 'I'll walk to the Dilly for some smokes, hang on.' Then she turned and left with an uncommon resignation in the way she poised her walk.

Brigitte waited almost forty-five minutes. Huldah came back, already high, and the traces of the disappearing humiliation still visible in her manner.

'So hard to get?' asked Brigitte and immediately fidgeted in her purse for money.

'Not smokes, Brigitte. The money. And I don't want yours.' She passed the reefer across. Brigitte took it, but bowed her head, and imagined how hard the money came.

'I couldn't do that, Huldah,' she said.

'I know, Brigitte. I know. I used to say the same.' Then she smiled and the hurt disappeared. 'I'm black. So they think they can be wild and primitive and dirty with me. They are. But I'm not. And I can't take the drudge of factories, and the creamy scum of offices. So what's left?'

Brigitte looked at Huldah's eyes, so clear, so honest, so different from those in the filth of the schools and factories, those who choose to live as if life were a slow way to die.

Huldah saw the thought and her face, serene now and accepting, broadened into a smile. 'So I guess I'm just about fucked, sister.' And Brigitte convulsed with laughter, broke from a restraint, touched her friend's hand, and stared into those depthless eyes that could consume pain, blink, and bring themselves back to smile. —O, the beautiful sin of pride. Who called it deadly? And before her thoughts turned to Jazz Murphy, Huldah reached across and touched Brigitte's chin, raised her face, and smiled with respect into the crying eyes.

'I want to, Huldah,' she said, 'It's stupid, but I need to set a ghost free.'

Each system works with adaptable variations to suit the blind, dark alleys of human nature. Along that street they hired a housekey and a roomkey from the room's agent, the landlord's ponce. Then they waited, and quickly a customer hired Brigitte's body. He was clean and well dressed, but stumbled a little drunkenly, and his body smelt of stale deodorants. He took Brigitte's body awkwardly, clumsily, with moments of innocent brutality, but without malice, and almost with apologies. And in the nonchalant trance that covered her, Brigitte almost gave him her pawned body. In that was the difference the customer never understood. Then Brigitte paid the rent to the streetponce, and pocketed the change. Slowly, with the elasticity of demand, the room rent increases, and the girl can take it or leave it. Or join the stable. Either way she earns no surplus value no more than she would at other work. The landlord rents, Brigitte pawns, and pays a premium for her deficiency; he earns a premium for his surplus. And only by imprisoning others in the same contradiction could she escape it.

But she escaped the experience of pawning her body. It fulfilled a promise, and gave an outward show to an inner belief.

Huldah, concerned and feeling guilty, walked alongside her. They reached the Dilly and drifted through the small, narrow back alley clustered with garbage bins. On the steps there small groups of boys and girls nodded on whatever they could afford to buy. Occasionally a drunk, misled, came and sat. Uniformed police, plain clothes police, male and female, saturated these alleyways, and under such surveillance, Brigitte and Huldah bought a handful of reefers and swayed back out into the crowds pushing towards the cinemas and theatres along the Haymarket.

Back in Brigitte's room they sat and smoked, but talked very little. No ghost had been set free in Brigitte's mind; but one had come alive in Huldah's. Silently, Brigitte and Huldah slept together in the room. They needed each other's company, needed to be alone and needed each other close by, also, to reach to, at any moment, for a touch of help, of understanding.

Days later Brigitte received a pay cheque and a dismissal notice in the mail. A rigmarole of employment offices, social security offices, supplementary benefit offices, relieved only by largatyl and reefers, followed a relentless grind of explanations to dim, context-less officials. Brigitte had no wish to talk to them and nodded here and there, signed her name, as required, without any show of pride, to them. In the evenings she danced at the Calendar Club with Huldah, and laughed, got stoned, and lay in bliss each time she went to bed. When the nights were not too cold, not far, far too cold, they sat on the backsteps of the Dilly and watched the people of the world go past the end of the alley. It was on such a night that Huldah took her first shot of heroin. When the needle left her arm she rose and danced forward on the backs of her heels, splayed out her hands in an act of magic, rocked on her heels, and fell. A woman police constable came forward from the shadows. She knelt over Huldah, pulled back the eyelids, lifted Huldah's hand and sniffed the syringe. Then into the radio on her lapel she said it's too late, no need to hurry. Then she gently composed Huldah's body on the ground. She looked at Brigitte and shook her head, sadly, with a mother's disappointment and compassion. Brigitte pushed past, scrambled past arms, raced into the Haymarket, through the crowds of strollers, and safely made the refuge of the subway station on the corner.

Nothing moved in Brigitte's life. With no Huldah, with no place to run to, nothing to run from, she sat and stared at the walls of her room, living on even less than the social security gave her. Sometimes she wandered about, almost as if the body rose itself and walked, and placidly she went with it. Often she sat in the library because its warmth was free, and the people there quiet and civilised when once within its confines. But if she read, she re-read the books of childhood and early adolescence, and enjoyed a secondhand pleasure, and reflections, from the joy the books had first given her. But the words school and teacher were words polluted and repulsive with sick connotations, and their presence in her mind were unacceptable, disgusting, unnecessary obscenities. Not because of the actions of one, or a number, but also for the visible results of the actions of so many that produced so many as warped and broken as she, Huldah, and the boys and girls on the steps everywhere in the night, ready and glad to leave this world behind, even if only for hours, and at the terrible cost that they regularly saw their brothers and sisters pay.

And yet, over the course of many books, a feeling of quarantined toleration set in, as if she were about to walk through a crowd of lepers and the diseased and disfigured, to rescue a child abandoned there, a child that might be further touched by them, and further sickened with their diseases. Pacified with largatyl, and with reefer smoke as a disinfectant, Brigitte set out to acquire an academic education. She was almost eighteen years of age and it was awkward and clumsy to acquire the habit of studying children's books. Each time she looked up from the pages of the correspondence courses she saw across at the other wall of her room the child, as in a dream, staring back at her with her own face. She smiled at herself through the smoke. Education is never free to adults, though they need it most. And Brigitte pawned her body here and there to acquire the wherewithal to buy from different schools as many courses on the same subjects as possible. The child's growth was slow and halting and started from zero, but slowly took on the form of an exponential curve, and she learned how to learn and how to think. It was slow and often ungainly, but finally it blossomed; and as a by-product Brigitte acquired the paper of diplomas. When Brigitte looked at the child now she saw her own twenty year old face, widely read and widely experienced, a strange stranger to others, but well and deeply known to herself, well and deeply knowing the others who saw her.

The same indifference that had led her to the libraries led her, casually, to seek work. And the Government labour office sent her to Ercole's. Brigitte liked it, gave up her room in the East End, and moved across London to the area of her work. Ercole was pleased. The labour office had unexpectedly sent him an artist who had displayed effort in training her talent. He understood, and gave her the liberty he allowed himself. He was a little of her and a little of Jazz Murphy. He needed, always, someone like himself forever close-by, and when their vitalities matched the best in him came forth without the slightest stutter in its utterance. He was a craftsman formed by the need to give beauty to his work. He knew the shadows that illuminate every smile, and the pains that no joys can ever destroy.

When Brigitte detected a kindred spirit in a face, and tried to brush it into prominence, Ercole re-brushed it back to tranquility. People do not even look at themselves in mirrors, never wonder at the thoughtless eyes staring back at them from a different time, knowing it is only a reflection, and knowing the reflection thought the same. Ercole would not hurt people by showing them their reality in celebratory photographs. He laughed with Brigitte, watching her widening eyes watching his, and asked what reality she wanted. The smooth, silken skin of a girl's buttocks, or an assful of pimples? And her free and roaring laughter made him feel he was not unwanted in the world, that he did serve a purpose. And all his silent, lonely battles in his exile, for and against the pursuit of the hopes old age had long ago made him abandon, now served a purpose in the service of this young Irish girl. All the cherished hopes he had thought forever lost he found again resting in her spirit, and in that found the ending of his life becoming satisfied. It is the peace of those who do not trouble to live or die when their final sickness comes. He taught Brigitte to spread the intensity of her love, and to give beauty to all, and experience the joy of that accomplishment, the rest and peace it brings to the soul to remember the once whispering beauty of the innocent child that lies buried, in marked and unmarked graves, in every adult. That uncurtailed love would live forever in Ercole, and he taught Brigitte to understand that it also lived in her.

She sucked on a plain cigarette and smiled at him. He smiled back, never suspecting the ganja smoke that lay behind the smile, and the agony that lay behind that. Ercole had fought the Ghost of unanswerable thoughts alone, and learned to co-exist with them peacefully, for most of the time. And Brigitte chaffed him with childish, daughterly play and made his eyes sparkle. Like the virgins of Finsbury comforting their lonely evenings with bars of chocolate, Ercole was mocked for his pleasure, his anticipatory pleasure of a book in the evening and a glass of brandy by his lonely bedside. Then she'd tell him he had taught her to think like that, and his laughing face would expand with fatherly joy. He was proud that she saw how calm life could be with a bar of chocolate, a book, and a glass of brandy; how peaceful and gentle these pleasures were. And Brigitte, behaving like an intelligent daughter to him, let him believe. It was better to deceive, to lie, than to break his loving heart. It was this that Ercole had unwittingly taught, and Brigitte was grateful for the graciousness of the lesson. Almost before she knew it, it had passed into her nature.

'There's an outside job today,' he remarked.

'Rent money?'

'Hmm.'

'O.K.' And they quietly carried on with their work. Rent money was the slob finding work of locating members of the public to pose for product advertisements. Each was promised a sum of money if selected from the trials. Then they were told they had failed. They hadn't. Brigitte and Ercole re-touched the photos and cleared out identifying, background details, and sent the results to the overseas agencies who added the products and the catch-lines, and produced the results in the local magazines. The system worked back, and no agency had to pay modelling fees. It paid the rent. And neither Ercole nor Brigitte had a conscience about paying their rents from the public's vanity. It wasn't an anti-English sentiment. Too many members of the English establishment paid their rents, and more, in a similar spirit. Overseas, their mirror images did the same.

'Tall, long-legged, lean, young, handsome basically. And male.'

'Where?' Brigitte feigned awe-struck excitement, 'I don't even care if he's stupid.'

'Our model, Brigitte, our model. Try the usual place.'

'I need money for a brandy,' she lied. Ercole nodded understandingly, and squeezed some notes into her hand. And Brigitte, haltered with cameras to reassure the victim, wandered down the street to the subway station, and slowly dissolved a capsule in her mouth. Then she rested her stretching back against the red, broad postbox outside the station, and waited. Again, the newsvendors' placards had changed their headlines. Another bomb had exploded on the London pavements, and twenty-six hostages had been released from the hi-jacked aircraft. Brigitte lacked the brave new logic of those who trusted their lives to machines, machines they controlled no more than they choose the beliefs of their chance nationality, and the subsequent loyalties that stemmed from it. Some — the exiles within — refused to trust their lives to that fate, and even those who did felt a disgust for the atrocity that mirrored the predicament of the world divided into groups of opposing patriots. The motives of the patriots are identical; love of their exclusive and idealised beliefs. And their cities are posted with their monuments to war and death.

Brigitte straightened quickly and moved to intercept the young man coming out of the station.

'Sir, I'm a representative of the B. K. Shepherd Advertising Studios. We're photographing young men for a product advertisement. Perhaps you'd be interested?'

He smiled, puzzled and taken aback, but his smile remained.

'You're Irish, aren't you?' And Brigitte, accustomed and equal to it, flashed back a quick, apologising smile.

'Yes. The only looney they can get for the job. I've been standing here all afternoon looking for someone suitable. And you're only the second I've seen in three hours. I'm about to call it quits. May I photograph you? The artistic director, Mr. Ercole, makes the final decision, and you'll be notified if you're selected.'

'Young lady, I'm quite sure that hundreds of suitable men have come out of that station in the last three hours.'

Brigitte smiled again and patted the cameras. 'Not when you look closely. We've even looked in all the model books, and no luck. It'll only take a few minutes and you might make a lot of money from it.'

'How much?'

'A few hundred, at least.'

'There's one condition.'

'Oh!'

'You'll come out with me tonight.'

'I'm sorry. That would compromise my position in the Company.'

'Forget the photo and come out anyway.' His face looked concerned, and it impressed Brigitte with its abrupt show of sincerity.

'Look. I was born in a place called Ireland, you already know that. And some of those with a loyalty to their birth mattress have been bombing London all day. They're not mine to own or dis-own. But it's your mattress they've been bombing, and you probably love every flea in it as much as they love theirs. So what would we talk about?'

He laughed, relieved, and reached out his hand to touch hers.

'Don't worry about that. I'm hijacked too.'

'You've just lost me.'

'I'm off the Jewish mattress.'

'Swop you any day.'

'Good. So let's go out tonight and swop.'

Brigitte eyed him for a moment. 'Fleas, you mean?'

His expression dropped more open than before, and his eyes sparkled as happily as a child's.

'Names. Let's start with names. Mine's Simon.'

'Brigitte.'

A pause came, and Brigitte tried to avoid his eyes and look around the street, and hide her smile. She fidgeted with the camera straps.

'Brigitte! You'll lose your job.' She looked up, bewildered. 'My photo for your Mr. Ercole.'

Brigitte flushed and stepped back, fumbling to grab a camera. She shrugged a gesture of embarrassed explanation, raised the viewfinder to her eye, brought him into focus, and smiled at his boyish happiness. He saw the smile behind the camera, and when he smiled back Brigitte photographed him.

Ercole was delighted. Brigitte had been less than twenty minutes, and brought back an ideal photograph of plain, sincere joy in a young man's face. Many would stop to look at such a photograph, and it would certainly help sell products on any continent.

'Oh Brigitte, my Brigitte,' he said, 'you're an artist, an artist. It is exquisite. It gives me joy. You captured the bird on the wing in still motion. Yet I swear it still swoops and dives, and rises again to the heavens. It is superb. A work of love, Brigitte. A work of love.'

Brigitte dragged on her cigarette and looked away.

'Ahh! You like him.'

'Yes, I do, Ercole. But give me some money for a little brandy and I'll go home and forget it.'

He seemed sad, or pitying, on her account, and put some money into her hand. 'You're a very lonely child, Brigitte. Believe me, I know how it hurts.'

'—O fuck off, Ercole,' she shouted against her will, and walked across the floorboards of the studio and out onto the street.

At one end of Queensway there's a street of all night shops and Greek, Italian, French and Chinese cafes and clubs. Brigitte went to the Basement Bistro, bought some ganja, and sat in the darkened, peaceful room, sipped sweet tea, and smoked. When common, everyday work took on the utility of prostitution, its usefulness ended. The physical and mental abilities of people are always available for hire. It is when those skills are pawned to expediency that prostitution enters, leaving the utility available to the highest bidder, however bankrupt of humanity the currency may be.

Silently, without any warning, a strong weariness swept along Brigitte's back, like an obituary she had once read. She laid her head on her arms folded on the table and slept.

The essence of that obituary was written by Stanley Milgram. It is a book called *Obedience to Authority.* Through a mesh to screen out psychopaths and sadists, he selected hundreds of normal people, postmen, doctors, tradesmen, clerks, typists, teachers and housewives to prove the connection between pain and learning. In Yale University they were given the job of teachers to normal, adult students. The adult students were being taught to pair words, dark-night, bright-day, good-bad. Electrodes were strapped to the hands of each student bound into his chair, and through those electrodes the punishment for wrong answers was inflicted. The teacher merely pressed a labelled button and a slap of electricity stabbed through the hands and ran into the body of the student. Starting at fifteen volts, and increasing by fifteen volts to four hundred and fifty volts, each button was labelled with the severity of the shock, from slight shock to hard shock to Danger: Severe shock. At shocks of seventy-five volts the adult students grunted with irrepressible pain. At one hundred and fifty volts they screamed and rolled their chairs over and squirmed on the floor and begged to be released. At three hundred and thirty volts they lay inert on the floor, their unconscious bodies convulting only when another shock was administered. Without encouragement of any kind, over sixty percent of the teachers continued to punish to the limit available in the controlled experiment: four hundred and fifty volts. In batch after batch of teachers, free to stop whenever they liked and still receive full pay, over sixty percent continued to the limit available to them in order to elicit correct answers from students punished beyond consciousness. The teachers were deliberately given no encouragement. After a teacher had administered three shocks of four hundred and fifty volts, each individual experiment was ended.

Mercifully, Professor Milgram's adult students were actors, and the behaviour of the 'teachers' the subject of the experiment. From the USA, to country after country, each experiment proved that never less than sixty percent of good men, good women, from a wide and diverse cross section of the native population, willingly tortured adults merely to teach them to say night in response to the conventional dark. But the teachers did not show anger, but genuine concern, over the slow progress of their tortured victims. Brigitte's mind twitched, and she awoke.

She paid and left the cafe, and wandered along the streets, browsing here and there, unconcerned and far away, and daydreaming of wordless, imageless thoughts. She climbed the steps of the Porchester Public Baths, pulled open the dirty door, and walked across the foyer to the ticket office. The woman looked up from her book, and smiled, again, a balm of ease. And the fixity of sadness in Brigitte's eyes broke from its tension. She smiled back.

'I was asked out today,' she said, before she knew she had spoken.

The woman winked. 'With the way they are nowadays, love, you better take your tablet and put on a crash helmet.' Brigitte bowed her head and laughed. 'A towel, shower, soap and shampoo, please.' The woman clicked the tickets off the machine. Brigitte thanked her, and tried for a moment to thank her more with her eyes. The woman winked again. 'Enjoy yourself, love,' she said, and went back to her book.

*

Jazz Murphy did not long remain an idle curiosity to the villagers. The transition from visitor to resident occurred without any growth of familiarity. Solitary, emotionally and intellectually independent, he contained their well-practised, wary prying into his past life with replies of aloft, polite humour. He was as canny as they; and that observation became the greater part of their judgement of him. It was the limit, also, of their dour, bedimmed judgement, and they missed the greater part of the man.

When the solemn eyes of the child Brigitte showed him her affinity her longing for the kinship of a kindred spirit, he accepted it with gratitude. And unwittingly returned a kindred affection. Wanderers often jostle into each other's way, smile for the immediately recognised affinity, and move to make room for each other. When they find that they are so much alike the room increases in size, beyond both of them, and they fill it with oddities of trust, privacy, and their own unique eccentricities; all invisible from the outside. But strangers feel it when they come into its presence. So it became with the villagers, who felt medieval and parsonic, in the uncanny presence of Brigitte and of Jazz Murphy, together. The villagers retreated into their dour reserve and watched.

The child Brigitte grew quiet, graceful, and serene, happy in her new world. And Jazz Murphy was industrious, serious, and frugal. It was the narrowness of the villager's judgement that gave these peripherals their importance. But that judgement was a bascule, and these peripherals its binding straps.

Jazz Murphy knew he lived in a singular state; a man not quite defined. He did not expect the villager's conclusions to be profound, nor conclusions reached by logical thought, nor any thought. Merely the conclusions mysteriously agreed upon across dining tables, bar counters, with no traceable signs other than casual remarks left hanging in silences and the meeting of eyes, nods of consent, and gestures of compliance from those who agree only to be agreeable, and the endlessly recurring abscissions that leave so much unsaid and contextless, so that it seems no more need be said. Yet a hint of depravity, of sexual exploitation, would have concurred with their unconscious conclusions, and resolved the mystery of the relationship between the adolescent girl and the adult man. It would have made all comprehensible to the confines and limits of their instincts. It was never spoken between them, but the sanctity of Brigitte's childhood, and of her adolescence, was not the adytum of her mind, but the virginity of her womb. This was a membrane respected and esteemed with primeval strength, and to protect it they would have sacrificed the holder, expected the holder to sacrifice herself, in many ways, for it.

Those who believe in a paradise not of this world, who believe in a justice not of this world, who believe in their life everlasting, but not in this world, will not hesitate long to destroy even humankind in order to preserve it, resurrected, in some other world where their god presides in supreme wisdom. And to such people a quirk of female anatomy easily becomes holy, becomes an essence of their morality, and yet, as in all their beliefs, remains not unspeakable, but mysteriously unquestionable.

Those who believe in this world as humankind's only habitat, will not press the electric, labelled buttons to destroy it. But those of them who would, would acknowledge themselves as psychopaths.

Closely, knowing the sleeping adult would remember better the whispers when she awoke from childhood, Jazz Murphy spoke to Brigitte of the pre-eminence of her sensibilities, her ever increasing consciousness of the joy of existence, and the ever increasing joy of that consciousness. Jazz Murphy enticed her to live in her time, her conception of the universe. Occasionally the open, sleeping eyes sparkled with insight, and a ghost of thought from her mind, as if she were about to awake, then slumbered, wide-eyed, again. When the adult dimly awoke, and poured forth the past of her childhood as if it were a dream, or a nightmare, but in every way the truth that guided the sleep-filled, stumbling adult, she did not believe, as her adolescent body lay in Jazz Murphy's arms, that the wounds of childhood would harness and control the adult long, long after the child had died. With the health and spring of bodily youth, she believed her vitality would overcome any obstacle in the way of full adulthood.

It was the night she and Jazz Murphy spent together in each other's arms, and the second-last time they ever met. Brigitte, in her radiance, wanted, with gleefulness, to defy the villagers. No hand that had touched her childhood would dare raise itself, again, in acknowledgement of the state of the adult. That hand would also have to claim responsibility for the wounds of the child, and surely that would shame them. Brigitte did not know that the master villagers would consider her defective material, unsuitable and better dead, like the children on the steps everywhere in the night. The squashing of so many like these the master villagers of the world never noticed. It was hardly a task, and they performed it with brute indifference.

Jazz Murphy was skilled, acute to the swell of emotions. Into Brigitte's rush of talk he dropped solitary words that guided the flow, made it whirl and foam, made it pause for moments, and helped it to ebb. Considered, conscious evil did not work in the mind of the villagers, nor in the mind of Brigitte. But neither accepted the innocence of the other. Brigitte, that night, scorned the evil of the villagers, and the villagers, forever, saw with their clear eyes of animal survival, how clean they wished to keep their master village.

Finally, during the last night together, Jazz Murphy surrendered to the enthusiasm of youth, agreed to leave the village for some other village in some other country, and promised to bring again the power of his presence, as he had before, on another fateful day, into the nervous austerity of Brigitte's home.

*

Brigitte, glowing with relaxation and freshness, walked easily from the baths. The lady in the ticket office smiled after her. It was good to see the beauty of health and youth unadorned and unspoilt by cosmetics and the Court-like vanity of marcelled hair. Brigitte's walk had the unassumed stature of a flower's stem, and swayed peacefully through the throngs of people rushing aside and past on the London pavements. She passed through the entrance hall of the subway station, and wondered at the lack of timidity, or embarrassment shown by the men and women who stood by the walls and waited, without demur, in the stand of natural selection demanded by the ritual of courtship. Transposed, they might have been a guilty queue waiting outside a brothel. Yet as Brigitte thought this she felt a sympathy, and a respect, for their plight. If sex drove them to this it was an indomitable demand, and they should be allowed to easily free themselves of it. But it was their individual loneliness, and their blinded inability to accept it as a force, that touched her heart.

Simon was sitting on one of the ancient, wooden benches with uncomfortably curved, slatted backs that stood along the platform. Brigitte sat beside him, and looked the other way, and smiled when he said hello, then slipped her hand into his. He thought it charming, and girlishly shy; and it was. He held her hand as if it were an angel's, and guided her onto the train. They left the subway at Notting Hill Gate, and walked back out into the evening light. Brigitte was happy to stroll along; happy, for a while to deceive herself. They walked in the direction of the park, and when the restaurants became less and less frequent, selected one and entered. The unsure delicacy of their relationship still hovered gently. They touched hands over the white linen of the tablecloth, past the vase and its solitary flower, past the uncorked, dark bottle of wine that waited, and the miniature coffee cups that waffed a foreign fragrance into the air. Each time Simon tried to speak Brigitte squeezed his hand, smiled, and looked away. The moment conversation settled, reality would intrude into this brief taste of romance. Lies about the past, about the present, lies to ease out a vista of a pleasant future, lies told to deny that impossibility, lies told to deny the transient nature of her happiness, lies told to prolong it, and to accommodate and avoid hurt, would spring like weeds into the relationship. Or she might tell the truth, sure that it too would startle him, and frighten him away.

'You're a very mysterious girl, Brigitte.'

She smiled. 'And I have great, big, clear brown eyes, hmm?'

'Cynic.' He lifted his hand away from hers and poured a glass of wine. She lowered her eyes as he raised it to his lips. He noticed the difference.

'Brigitte! How else can I get past the convent school veils?'

'Oh Simon,' she said with great innocence, 'I never knew boys went to convent schools.' He began to choke on the wine and struggled to empty the glass. 'Brigitte!'

'And I can scream and kick and say Angel, Jesus Jesus, swifter, faster, svifter-vasser, svifter-fassar in English, Irish, Latin and eighteen other unique and homeric languages.'

She held his startled and bemused gaze, without smiling, watching the deepening of their understanding of their relationship. And the evening passed on as they playfully explored each other, and Brigitte parried his curiosity about her previous life, her years in London, and her expectations of life. Simon, in his placid, middle-class ease, all his battles always behind him, his steady, daily obligations no burden, looked on Brigitte's life as a fascinating adventure that made her gallant, and a little unsteady, but attractively so. A small knot of reserve within Brigitte remained untouched, but recognised and respected.

Brigitte watched the change as Simon turned from admirer to partisan. Soon he would be her lover, and they would lie together, and afterwards she would tell him whom he loved.

*

Jazz Murphy walked back and forth outside his rented home. Not far away on the island the armies were fighting. Well behaved, well disciplined young men and women were maiming and killing each other, and others even more innocent than themselves. The identical causes of the armies were so great, so much more important than they, that all ties of human kinship were ignored, and each killed the other because he alone ignored human kinship.

The evening dimmed towards night. Jazz Murphy felt again the soundless presence of strangers approach. Each time he reached the gable wall he paused and turned back before the corner. Surely they would, sooner or later, seize that opportunity to attack. Earlier that day a group of male villagers had pushed him out of Brigitte's home while he listened to her screams under her father's wrath and the chastising smacks of deliberating punishment. Surely the villagers would seize the opportunity to attack him now as he turned his back at each corner. And surely that would divide their forces, and give him a chance to reduce their numbers, before the inevitable beating began.

He was halfway along the length of the house when two hooded men stepped out from the corner. He turned and saw another two approaching. Refusing the useless and humiliating opportunity to run, he kicked and punched when they merged around him and attacked. Then they carried the unconscious body into the house and laid it on the kitchen table. All but one left, and disappeared into the darkness of the fields. Inside the house the knife flashed, and did its work. But not to kill. And in peasant style a fist beat on the village doctor's door, a message was murkily whispered. The doctor sighed, left his book and his brandy, and drove to Jazz Murphy's rented home.

*

That was many years before this night, as Brigitte and Simon walked back towards Notting Hill Gate, strolled, looked in shop windows, lingered about the pavement to prolong the still enchantment of the evening, and wandered on, arm in arm.

They passed-by pub after pub, each one too crowded and too noisy with alcoholic trivialities to be entered. Throughout the world each pub is a village pub, and their habitues sincerely believe in their drunken, masterful solutions to the daily problems that confound science, any science. And in the islands off the west coast of the European continent almost every pub is structurally divided into class divisions, and the insularity of the intoxicated peasantry is jovial, expansive and content. They are also as dangerous as any village pub, where any odd word may cut against the grain of the villagers' received beliefs and their alcoholic certainty. Yet they are snug and inviting, and finally irresistible to a couple wandering home and dallying with the sweetness of the evening. When they entered the lounge bar Simon moved unfaltering and sure and indifferent to the element. No sense of strange animals' presence altered his casual behaviour. Brigitte, too, seemed indifferently relaxed, but cowed inside and listened to the vibrations as they drummed on the stoned cover of her feelings. The vibrations rang too hard, and disturbed her inner peace. She asked Simon to buy her a coffee, then slipped away to the toilets. In the cubicle she chewed one more capsule and swallowed its powder with her saliva. Another layer of cover draped over her. She rested her back against the squat cistern and smoked one more reefer, gigglish to the thought that anyone might smell the burning ganja. —O, for the gentleness of her people, and Brown Sugar, and their presence on the back steps of the Dilly. But first she would drink the coffee, ask Simon to leave with her, but leave alone if necessary.

When she returned to the bar Simon was sitting on the edge of a semicircular couch and exchanging conversation with a woman, some years older than Brigitte, and her friends. Simon obviously knew them all. He stood up and let Brigitte sit on the inside, then squeezed himself onto the edge of the seat. There was no coffee on the table. Simon noticed her gaze.

'They don't serve coffee in the evenings. I thought you'd like a glass of wine for a change.'

Brigitte had been drinking coffee all evening, and now she looked at the poison on the table. What could it matter. She raised the glass to her lips and sipped.

'I say, Simon,' the woman said and hiccupped, 'You've always been too fond of quiet little strays.'

'Of course, Violet. But you know I've always abhorred the loud-mouthed.'

'Oh dear. Have I said something wrong!'

'Brigitte, let me introduce you. This is Violet, and Paul, her boyfriend I believe. And Basil and Dorothy.'

Smiles were exchanged. Brigitte whispered hello, and reached for her glass. Violet flushed with drunken triumph. 'And Irish, Simon! Splendid! Tell me, Bridie, are you from Northern Ireland or from Eire?'

'You don't happen to speak Irish, do you, Violet?' Brigitte asked.

'But of course not, dearie.'

'I was born in southern Eire, Violet, not northern Eire. I'm sorry. You confused me.'

'Good gracious, Bridie. What on earth are you talking about.'

'I said you confused me, Violet. But no more than you would confuse a German if you asked her if she came from Eastern Germany or from Deutschland.'

'Clever little bitch, aren't you.'

'Violet's had a few too many, I'm afraid.' Paul tried to rally bravely and laughed. Violet ignored him.

'I hope you didn't spend all that time in the toilet planting a bomb, Bridie.'

'VIOLET!' And Simon spread his hands open in an appeal for peace.

'I know these Irish, Simon.' Violet hiccupped again. 'I see their stupid little faces in class every day.'

Brigitte tried to stand. Simon pressed on her shoulder.

'Violet, I want you to apologise to Brigitte.'

'Oh Simon you are so divinely naive. But please take your Irish bitch somewhere else.'

'And you will apologise to me, now.'

Violet inhaled a long draw on her long, filter-tipped cigarette. It seemed to calm her, and she blew a cloud of smoke across the table.

'You've certainly put yourself over a barrel, Moshe,' she said, 'Or should I say a barrel of oil? But even that's better than a bar of soap, wouldn't you think?' She tapped the ash from the cigarette and stared at him. 'I haven't the slightest intention of apologising to anyone.'

The fixity of Brigitte's eyes also stared across the table. Customers in the bar had turned, discreetly, to watch. And in the pause of the impasse, Brigitte's voice seemed to pluck tenderly at the silence.

'Why are you jealous of me, Violet?' she asked.

'JEALOUS! Of you! Good God I wouldn't have Simon even if he begged.'

'Then what is it, Violet? Why do I frighten you? What threat am I to you?'

'None at all, Bridie. You flatter yourself.'

'I doubt it, Violet. Women like you reduce everything to the level of their knickers. You must. It's the sole reason for your existence, after you've fed your mouth.'

'Please don't try to be educated, Bridie. It's very Protestant; and that isn't quite you, is it.'

'Not at all me, Violet. I think the jibbering syllogisms of popery always too automorphic, don't you?'

'I'm sure I haven't the faintest idea what you're trying to say.'

'No, of course not, Violet.' Brigitte smiled, and spoke slowly, 'you're just another typically stupid conceited English bitch.'

The noises and murmurs of the bar tilted in their aspect, and hushed almost to silence. Violet tried to ignore the fixity of hate in Brigitte's smiling eyes, and glanced quickly around the bar, claiming the assured empathy of her nationals. Simon's fingers gently caressed the nape of Brigitte's neck as he tried to relax her. The nerves sprung free and Brigitte's head twisted sharply as her shoulders and her back straightened.

'—O JESUS I HATE YOU!'

Violet, her face strained and tight-lipped, continued her expecting survey around the bar.

'Listen to me, Violet. I hate you. Understand me, you sow, I hate you. I hate you and I hate your kind—'

'Brigitte please Brigitte,' Simon tried to hold and caress her shoulders. She stood. 'Please, Brigitte, this isn't the place.'

'This *is* the place. This is where my chance nationality makes me a hostage to every idiot's bigotry and spite, and the love-the-underdog British keep as quiet as frightened, nazi-terrorised Germans. This is where the word Irish brings immediately the labelled response stupid. This is where I ought to wear a yellow shamrock when I dare to walk on the street. This is where sycophantic patriotism is a virtue, the culture of the masses.'

'Come Brigitte. Brigitte. They're not worth it.' Simon pleaded.

'Violet, you sow, your kind taught even the Anglo-Irish to despise you. You. Your kind. Even Wilde ridiculed your sham of manners, Shaw scorned you — Behan threw your own shit in your faces and you lapped it all up like demented imbeciles.'

Her breath rose and fell, too high and too deep to continue as her body heaved in its anger.

'Brigitte. Please. For me.'

'Well now you know, Violet. Now you fuckingwell know.'

Simon put his arm over her shoulders and hugged her to him, and she allowed him to walk her to the door and out onto the street. The bar remained quiet, and Violet, the centre of the silent attention, stared into her empty glass.

'Actually,' said Basil, with a resigned sadness and a little bravery, 'Actually, my grandmother was Irish, you know.' The atmosphere of the bar slipped back to normal and fresh rounds of drinks were posted on the tables.

Outside in the street, Simon stood and held the trembling Brigitte.

'This is the end, Simon. I can take no more. But I've wanted to shout at them for so long, all the interchangeable patriots, and their hatred for their own mirror images. They are everything they profess to hate. And they rule the world. There is no place where I can ever find refuge from them.'

He kissed her forehead, lay his forehead against hers and tried to ease her pain. 'Come home with me, Brigitte. We'll toast bread over the electric fire and drink tea in the dark. And make believe we're alone on some idyllic planet.'

'I need solitude, Simon,' she whispered, whispering to herself, 'I need a solitude I've never been able to find in life. I want to be away from people, away from beliefs. I want to lie for a thousand years in the earth, alone.'

For a moment they stood silent, then stepped slowly along the quiet streets, past the glowing joviality of the pubs, and the restaurants radiating the quiet contentment of candlelight, and the darkness of the night their comfort and confederate.

*

The blood soaked into his clothes and small rivulets of it moved eyelessly over the table and fell, drop by drop, onto the floor. There the pools expanded, and the urgency of the doctor's movements smeared the pools into streaks and twists as his feet hurried about the table. Long after he was gone the blood dried. It was Jazz Murphy's life blood, and the stains on the floor a picture of those petty wounds that are too cruel to kill their victims, and cleanly, inexorably, make life a hysterical, unendurable nightmare. And a living hell is never better than the peaceful void of death. And if death is not a euphemism for a concept too grotesque for sane contemplation; if the dead, too, are sensible to pleasure or pain, still there is nothing lost in the venture into death from a life of pain. Jazz Murphy had lived a life of unhurried hope, avoiding fools and foolish things, and drawing his strength from the occasional bouts of joy his work and hopes brought him. The petty wound that now cowered him with pain in his chair by the fire had the glee and spite of an idiot's sneer. And it sapped his life-force as surely as it had sapped his blood.

Brigitte stood by the door, the dried blood under her feet as she listened to Jazz Murphy talk into his glass of whiskey. She understood nothing of the philosophy his drunken ramblings tried to disentangle, and seemed to succeed. And the child and the woman in Brigitte was willing to hold fast until the turmoil broke and eased, until she could come gently forward, and touch, and comfort; sure she could give nourishment to the fallowed mind, and tend it back to health, and again join her happiness in its bloom.

He emptied the whiskey bottle into his glass, raised himself with the vigour of a youth, and flung the bottle hard against the wall. To Brigitte it was a small tantrum to bear, if only it would pass. She closed her eyes for a moment to gain strength, then crossed the room and knelt beside his chair. Her head lay over and rested against his arm, and soon his arm moved, moved slowly over her head, and rested on her shoulder. Brigitte relaxed, and sighed with relief, sure that mellowness, and then a rallying to health, would follow. His mumblings changed their harsh notes, his fingers softly caressed her shoulder and her hands caught at his hand and held it to her face. For the final moments of their time they stayed together that way.

When he spoke the words were clear, and freed of drunken slurring. Each word seemed to hang alone in the air, leave a meaning, then evaporate, and the words together formed yet another, complementary meaning. And while the individual, soft words dimmed the hysteria of the young girl, together they bonded to her the need to flee. The action of the villagers was easy to understand, if you had no illusions about the nature of humankind. The disciples of evil have never acted under its banner, for its greater glory, and never believed the banners they believed in were banners of evil. Jazz Murphy explained how the villagers had viewed him, how they viewed Brigitte, and why she must now desert, for her own solitude, those whose values she had revealingly betrayed. And leave, also, Jazz Murphy. Whatever was idealised in their relationship was fanciful; an unclean veil over the clean nature of their affinity. But Jazz Murphy's affinity was now turned to his compact with the universe, to his escape from pain, and his release of Brigitte to pursue her own hopes.

She took the money he folded into her hand, and gripped his hand with hers, knowing he was already infinitely remote from her. She rose and left the house. Outside, her strength dissolved in the void of purpose that faced her. She walked mutely into her parents' house and awaited the news of Jazz Murphy's fate. When it came she contrived another excuse and, deliberately coatless, set out for the mirage of London.

Inside the rented house darkened against the day by the window drapes, Jazz Murphy drank more whiskey, and even more, beyond the point of stupor, and eased himself from pain into death. The first touch of the blade against his wrist did not hurt. A moment later the warm pain screamed and threatened to defeat the limit of endurance. He cut again, then raised the blade to the left side of his neck, pushed it into the skin, and pulled it across his throat.

*

Startled, Simon sat up in bed. 'Holy Jesus, Brigitte! What had they done to him?'

Lying back disinterested on the pillow, and gazing at the ceiling as she talked, Brigitte almost smiled at Simon's alerted concern.

'They'd cut his balls off, Simon. Like they'd geld a horse.'

'Jesus!'

'He could have lived with that. It was the burden he would have been to me that broke him.'

'But it's barbaric, Brigitte.'

'Analysing things, Simon, and naming them, doesn't stop or cure the fucking things, you know.'

'Yes, but surely someone protested.'

'Surely, Simon. Surely. Someone protested.' Then she turned over, half bored, half wanting sex, but disappointed that he did not see that justice and injustice are merely points of view. Common observation should have told him that. Milgram brought into focus what history had already written. And Brigitte was beyond the point of patience that can explain that virtue and vice come to nothing, but if they have potency to their believers they have none elsewhere, and viewed from there are merely the expediences of cynicism. It is their blindness to this that makes their names so unendurable when questions concerning the adytum of life, and its wraith, are proposed.

'I have to go now, Simon.' She smiled at his wide eyes that held so much tenderness for her.

'We could stay together, Brigitte,' he said. 'We could clean a space between us and make something decent of it.'

Her face beside his laughed into his eyes, and for a moment she loved him, again, for the innocence of his bouncing, racing, boyish optimism. It reminded her of someone she once knew in herself, of the early days of Jazz Murphy's company, of the hopeful days of paintings and talk, of the exquisite nights of books, and that other time in that private universe, where she moved in her time, a karma spirit in the universe.

'I'm going home, Simon.'

'Then promise me that.'

'Promise what?'

'That you will go home. Nothing more. That you won't do anything to hurt yourself.'

'O.K., Simon. I promise.' She looked at him again, and kissed his concerned eyes. Then with a smooth urgency slipped on her clothes, ignored Simon's talk, kissed him again, and left. The contexts of their worlds were so different that the words of their common vocabulary exchanged totally different meanings. Brigitte understood that, understood that Simon did not, and could not, and his innocence encapsulated the world's. And Brigitte was mute because she was languageless on a strange planet, merely sensing what the inhabitants said, and unable to reply. Living hurt her, and life was not a home to her.

Nor were the streets outside, but they were dark and empty and comfortable to stroll through. It was near to peacefulness to linger along the night streets, to pass the yellow glow of the lamps, to let her face touch the chill of the air, to wander through the insignificance of the universe, to smile for its gentleness, to know she was an exile within herself, to know that longing, finally, had disappeared. No more the ecstasy of paint and canvas, the wild and beautiful talk, the vibrant thoughts and the books that tried so deeply to make sense of the meaningless of the universe, and so transcended the meaningless, only to find they had become incommunicably exiled to the concerns of the world, become its failures, misfits, eccentrics, and those Brigittes whose minds were oceans of broken fragments, calmed and illuminated within, but still oceans of broken fragments within and as silently threatening to her sanity as her thoughts of the galaxies of the night sky in the arenaless universe.

She left the maze of narrow streets and turned towards Westbourne Grove and its all night bistros and supermarkets. The street was quiet and the bistros subdued and curtained. She knew the scene well and knew that in the darkened cul-de-sac at Chepstow Road a police van waited. Sometimes an empty, cruising taxi changed frequency, and police mysteriously appeared to support those who cruised, un-uniformed, in old, battered cars along the silent streets. Only the down-at-heel pushers, users themselves, worked from the darkened doorways. And what they had to sell was always suspect. The bistros had better reputations, and more safety, but higher prices. Brigitte walked slowly, near the kerb, in street walker fashion. The odd taxis and odd battered cars that passed paid no attention to the oldest profession.

'Brigitte! sas parakalo, ella.' Brigitte smiled. She knew the Cypriot, and his ignorant arrogance. He was cowering in a doorway on the other side of the street. She walked across.

'How's life?' she asked, without bothering to smile. She knew him, and knew his kind. They were the easiest pushers to handle, so long as you never allowed them to handle you, not even with the slightest word, nor any of their frequent gestures.

'Brigitte, I have good stuff. Really good.'

'I don't use any anymore, Yanni. I'm going to get married, become a domestic servant, have children, and get a repeat script for Librium or something.'

'I'll sell you twenty for ten pounds.'

'Fuck off.' She turned and walked back across the street.

'No, Brigitte, no. Not Librium.' He crossed the street after her and shoved his hand in front of her. 'Look!' His hand was full of two-toned capsules, yellow over brown, without markings. Brigitte looked from his trembling hand to his streetworn clothes and the fight for dignity that struggled in his eyes.

'They're homemade rubbish, Yanni.'

'No, Brigitte, no. I swear. Hong Kong. They're the best. Made in Hong Kong.'

'I'll give you ten for fifty.'

He froze; and smirked. 'You're dirt. Dirt.'

She turned away and walked into the all-night supermarket. She picked up cans, read the labels, put them down again, slowly killing time. It amused her, the thought of killing time slowly in this universe. Yanni was still outside. Brigitte bought a can of orange juice, camembert, two bread rolls, and a bottle of cough syrup.

Yanni stood in her way as she passed out of the shop. He still had a mediterranean scowl sulking on his face, and threatening. Brigitte opened her carrier-bag. 'Count them in, Yanni.'

From his pockets he took handfuls of the capsules and counted them into the bag in twos and threes. A lot were probably dummies, but Brigitte handed him the money and Yanni disappeared back to his shadows along the street. Brigitte walked the other way, up the Chepstow Road and turned left into the gaunt, spectral slums. She stopped at the antique shop just past the corner, its windows and interior a dumping ground for ancient painting, and the struggling copies of the masters the ambitious had tried to learn from. She reached into her bag, took some capsules, and swallowed them. Then she sipped a little of the cough mixture. She thought about the room in the house three streets away. There was nothing in it to identify her. Life has no significance, but it has utility. It is a receptacle for joy, or sorrow. And death, also, only has utility. Brigitte smiled, for herself, for the devout aspirations of the painting, for the dirt of the street, and the dark sky that sheltered the city. Accuse them, Father, for they know not what they do.

The thought came strangely to Brigitte. She had no wish to hurt, nor any regret for the leaving of a life others had condemned, continuously, from the moment of her birth, as they tried, without evil, to mould her with their values, and make her happy.

Already the drugs were working the magic, and she felt the ocean of broken fragments in her mind begin to connect, and piece together a coherent resignation and acceptance for the mistake of her existence. It would be nice to merely fade into nothingness, the utility of death. The capsules were good, and less than fifty would certainly kill. Brigitte laughed at the context of her vocabulary, took some more capsules, and wandered along the street. Tomorrow, Brigitte would be gone, and the universe not one atom more or less. And Brigitte's body, unclaimed, would go to the dissecting rooms of some medical school. And from there into smoke, and come back to the earth with the rains. It was so placid and peaceful to contemplate. It had the sweetness of eternity, until the sun cooled and the earth froze, and disappeared into a black door in space.

She took another capsule and held another in the palm of her hardened hand. These capsules would carry her into space. Take this, all of you, and drink from it. This is blood of my blood, flesh of my flesh. The words of transubstantiation learned in childhood. Accuse them, for they know not what they do. All those who teach, all those who rule the world.

Brigitte stopped by a lamp-post, put her arms about it and swung herself around. —O, the happiness. But if the god they preach is real she would toss into his face the mockery of life he had given her. He could punish, but never remove the wish from its brief existence.

Brigitte sat against the lamp-post and put the insane thoughts of insane humankind out of her mind. In an hour she would not be human. —O, the joy. To journey into space with the capsules, to journey into its freedom, to meet her forming unity with the universe.

She wanted to stay on the street, sit against the lamp-post, and contemplate the moon and the stars, an exile watching as the lights of the frontier drew nearer. Soon she would be home.

Brigitte returned to her room, swallowed the capsules, the syrup, and the camembert and bread that would hold them in her stomach. Then she lay down on the bed. Thoughts of infinite beauty, questionless and needless of answers, weaved through the brightening gem of consciousness. She slept, and consciousness passed from her and disappeared into the universe.

WOLFHOUND PRESS FICTION

Publishers of 'some of the most revolutionary recent fiction in Ireland' *from Rooney Prize for Irish Literature Citation for the 1983 award won by Dorothy Nelson's 'In Night's City'.*

DOROTHY NELSON
In Night's City — a novel

'Utterly compelling . . . a magician with language and with atmosphere'   Clare Boylan, RTE Review

NIALL QUINN
Voyovic, Brigitte and Other Stories

'the whole book has the effect of astonishing originality' *John Jordan, Irish Independent.* Niall Quinn was awarded the 'Brendan Behan Memorial Fellowship' for 1983.

MICHAEL MULLEN
Kelly — a novel

'certainly the funniest fantasy I have ever read' *Fantasy Today, USA.* 'Its ancestors include *The Crock of Gold,* the grotesqueries of *Finnegans Wake,* even *Jurgen*'   *Punch*

LIAM LYNCH
Shell, Sea Shell — a novel

'A book of great power and insight — a courageous work' *Sunday Independent.* 'A superb piece of writing . . . profoundly satisfying' *Irish Democrat.*

SAM BANEHAM
The Cloud of Desolation

'clever and imaginative essay into apocalypse fiction — an author well worth reading' *Sunday Independent*

HUGH FITZGERALD RYAN
The Kybe: A novel of Ireland in Napoleonic times.

A historical romance and a skilled, detailed and imaginative recreation of a whole community.

TOM McCAUGHREN
Run with the Wind

A classic novel of nature and survival — this book is the *Watership Down* of the fox world. Illustrated by Jeanette Dunne.

MERVYN WALL
Hermitage — a novel

'A compelling fable of the Ireland of yesterday. Mervyn Wall knows his Dubliners' *Irish Press*. 'A wise as well as an enthralling read' *Sunday Press*.

MARGARET BARRINGTON
David's Daughter, Tamar

'Tantalising, telling glimpses of several families' *Irish Times*. 'Her art is to compress and condense while suggesting acres to the imagination' *Irish Observer*. Introduced by William Trevor.

LIAM O'FLAHERTY

'A great, great writer, unique in any language, any culture ... He has all the potential of becoming a matrix for the yearnings of another generation' Neil Jordan, *Hot Press*.

Novels: *Famine, Skerrett, The Assassin, The Black Soul, The Wilderness, The Ecstasy of Angus.*

Stories: *Short Stories by Liam O'Flaherty (The Pedlar's Revenge and Other Stories).*

Autobiography: *Shame the Devil.*